Agile Software Development with Scrum

Ken Schwaber and Mike Beedle

SERIES IN AGILE SOFTWARE DEVELOPMENT

Robert C. Martin, Series Editor

PRENTICE HALL

Upper Saddle River, New Jersey 07458

Library of Congress Cataloging-in-Publication Data
  Agile Software Development with Scrum/Schwaber K.,
  Beedle M. Adff   p. cm.
  Includes bibliographical references index.   ISBN 0-13-
  067634-9 1. Scrum,
  Software Development. 2. Agile Software Methods. I.
  Title.

  512'–dc21   2001
  QA814.G27   00-055035   CIP

VP and Editorial Director, ECS: *Marcia J. Horton*
Publisher: *Alan R. Apt*
Associate Editor: *Toni D. Holm*
Editorial Assistant: *Patrick Lindner*
VP and Director of Production and Manufacturing, ESM: *David W. Riccardi*
Executive Managing Editor: *Vince O'Brien*
Managing Editor: *David A. George*
Production Editor: *Sarah E. Parker*
Composition: *PreTeX, Inc.*
Director of Creative Services: *Paul Belfanti*
Creative Director: *Carole Anson*
Art Director: *Heather Scott*
Art Editor: *Greg Dulles*
Manufacturing Manager: *Trudy Pisciotti*
Manufacturing Buyer: *Lisa McDowell*
Senoir Marketing Manager: *Jennie Burger*

Prentice Hall

© 2002 by Prentice Hall
Prentice-Hall, Inc..
Upper Saddle River, NJ 07458

Printed in the United States of America
20 19 18 17 16 15 14 13

ISBN 0-13-067634-9

Pearson Education Ltd., *London*
Pearson Education Australia Pty. Ltd., *Sydney*
Pearson Education Singapore, Pte. Ltd.
Pearson Education North Asia Ltd., *Hong Kong*
Pearson Education Canada, Inc., *Toronto*
Pearson Educacíon de Mexico, S.A. de C.V.
Pearson Education—Japan, *Tokyo*
Pearson Education Malaysia, Pte. Ltd.

Foreword

"Work can and should be an ennobling experience." So begins *Scrum – Agile Software Development*, one of the sanest and most practical books on agile software processes.

Software process is one of the hot topics of this decade. We've seen processes like XP, Adaptive, Crystal Clear, RUP, etc. We've seen the formation of the Agile Alliance; a group of experts dedicated to the promotion of people-oriented software processes that work without getting in the way. We've seen the creation of a commercial product based upon nothing but process. And we've seen dozens, if not hundreds, of books, lectures, classes, and articles extolling the virtues of one process or another.

In the midst of this hubbub, Ken Schwaber and Mike Beedle bring us Scrum. Scrum is an agile software development method with a proven track record. In this book you will read how the method was created, and some stories of the projects that made use of it. You'll read about how the authors battled to create a method that helped them get projects done in the presence of rapidly changing requirements. You'll read about what worked and what didn't, the problems they had, and the way they solved them. You'll read about how you can adapt their work to your particular needs.

Mike and Ken are uniquely qualified to author this book. Both have been active in the software industry for decades. Mike has been a manager of many software projects, and runs a successful software consultancy. Mike has fought the process battles many times. He knows what works and what doesn't. Ken has been involved with software process for a large portion of his career. He defined and built a software product that automated heavyweight software processes and created the methodology automation industry. From this experience he learned that such processes were not amenable to creating software in real market environments. But that's a story you can read in the book. Ken is a well-known management consultant who has helped dozens of project teams reach their goals.

This is a book for executives, software managers, project leaders, and programmers. It describes, in no uncertain terms, how each of these roles can apply the simple but effective principles and techniques of Scrum.

If you have to get a project done, and you want to use a process that helps you when you need help, and gets out of the way when you don't, then you should read this book. It is liable to be the catalyst of an ennobling experience.

Robert C. Martin

Foreword

When I finished at my grammar school at 18 I spent a year working in industry before going to University. My career direction at the time was electrical engineering, and in my year I learned a great deal about the engineering approach to building things. When I left university and entered the world of software development I was attracted to graphical modeling methodologies, because they helped put engineering discipline into software development.

At the heart of the engineering approach is a separation of design and construction, where construction is the larger part of the job and is a predictable process. Over time I began to find that this separation wasn't really useful for my software work. Doing the separation required too many tasks that didn't seem to really contribute to producing software. Furthermore, the construction part of the task wasn't really that predictable, and the design portion was much longer than the engineering approach assumed.

In Chapter 2 Ken describes a particular moment that brought this question home for him, when he spend time with DuPont's process engineering experts. There he learned the difference between defined and empirical processes, and realized that his software development needed to be controlled using an empirical approach.

We aren't the only ones who've been asking these questions about the nature of software development. Over the last few years there's been increasing activity in the area of what is now called Agile Methodologies, a new breed of software processes which are based on an empirical approach to controlling a project.

And software projects do need to be controlled. For many people, moving away from defined processes means descending into chaos. What Ken learned at DuPont was that a process can still be controlled even if it can't be defined. What Ken and Mike have written here is a book that shows you one way of doing that. Practices such as sprints, scrum meetings, and backlogs are techniques that many people using Scrum have used to control projects in chaotic circumstances.

In the future, we'll see more need for Scrum and the future developments built upon it. Software development has always been difficult to control. Recent studies indicate that the average project takes twice as long to do as its initial plans. At the heart of Scrum is the notion that if you try to control an empirical process with a system designed for defined processes, you are doomed to fail. It's becoming increasingly apparent that a large proportion of software projects are empirical in nature and thus need a process like Scrum. If you're running a project, or buying software, with difficult and uncertain requirements in a changing business world, these are the kinds of techniques you need.

Martin Fowler

Preface

This book was written for several audiences. Our first audience is application development managers that need to deliver software to production in short development cycles while mitigating the inherent risks of software development. Our second audience is the software development community at large. To them, this book sends a profound message: *Scrum represents a new, more accurate way of doing software development that is based on the assumption that software is a new product every time that it is written or composed.* Once this assumption is understood and accepted, it is easy to arrive at the conclusion that software requires a great deal of research and creativity, and that therefore it is better served by a new set of practices that generate a self-organizing structure while simultaneously reducing risk and uncertainty.

Finally, we have also written this book for a general audience that includes everyone involved in a project where there is constant change and unpredictable events. For this audience Scrum provides a general-purpose project management system that delivers, while it thrives on change and adapts to unpredictable events.

Software as "new product" as presented in this book, is radically different from software as "manufactured product", the standard model made for software development throughout the last 20 years. Manufacture-like software methods assume that predictability comes from defined and repeatable processes, organizations, and development roles; while Scrum assumes the process, the organization, and the development roles are emergent but statistically predictable, and that they arise from applying simple practices, patterns, and rules. Scrum is in fact much more predictable and effective than manufacturing-like processes, because when the Scrum practices, patterns and rules are applied diligently, the outcome is always: 1) higher productivity, 2) higher adaptability, 3) less risk and uncertainty, and 4) greater human comfort.

The case studies we provide in this book will show that Scrum doesn't provide marginal productivity gains like process improvements that yield 5-25% efficiencies. When we say Scrum provides higher productivity, we often mean several orders of magnitude higher i.e. several 100 percents higher. When we say higher adaptability we mean coping with radical change. In some case studies, we present cases where software projects morphed from simple applications in a single domain to complex applications across multiple domains: Scrum still managed while providing greater human comfort to everyone involved. Finally, we show through case studies that Scrum reduces risk and uncertainty by making everything visible *early and often* to all the people involved and by allowing adjustments to be made *as early as possible.*

Throughout this book we provide 3 basic things: 1) an understanding of why this new thinking of software as new product development is necessary, 2) a thorough description of the Scrum practices that match this new way of thinking with plenty of examples, and 3) a large amount of end-to-end case studies that show how a wide range of people and projects have been successful using Scrum for the last 6 years.

This last point is our most compelling argument: The success of Scrum is overwhelming. Scrum has produced by now billions of dollars in operating software in domains as varied as finance, trading, banking, telecommunications, benefits management, healthcare, insurance, e-commerce, manufacturing and even scientific environments.

It is our hope that you, the reader of this book, will also enjoy the benefits of Scrum, whether as a development staff member wishing to work in a more predictable, more comforting, and higher producing environment, or as a manager desiring to finally bring certainty to software development in your organization.

Thanks to our reviewers: Martin Fowler, Jim Highsmith, Kent Beck, Grant Heck, Jeff Sutherland, Alan Buffington, Brian Marick, Gary Pollice, and Tony D'Andrea. Ken would like to thank Chris, Carey, and Valerie. Mike would like to thank Laura, David, Daniel, and Sara. Together, we would like to thank our editors at Prentice Hall, Alan Apt and Robert Martin, as well as Jeff Sutherland for his many contributions to Scrum, and Kent Beck for demanding that we write this book.

Mike Beedle, Chicago
Ken Schwaber, Boston

Contents

List of Tables

List of Figures

CHAPTER 1

Introduction

"In today's fast-paced, fiercely competitive world of commercial new product development, speed and flexibility are essential. Companies are increasingly realizing that the old, sequential approach to developing new products simply won't get the job done. Instead, companies in Japan and the United States are using a holistic method; as in rugby, the ball gets passed within the team as it moves as a unit up the field." (Reprinted by permission of *Harvard Business Review* From: "The New New Product Development Game" by Hirotaka Takeuchi and Ikujiro Nonaka, January, 1986. Copyright 1986 by the Harvard Business School Publishing Corporation, all rights reserved.) —

This book presents a radically different approach to managing the systems development process. Scrum implements an empirical approach based in process control theory. The empirical approach reintroduces flexibility, adaptability, and productivity into systems development. We say "reintroduces" because much has been lost over the past twenty years.

This is a practical book that describes the experience we have had using Scrum to build systems. In this book, we use case studies to give you a feel for Scrum-based projects and management. We then lay out the underlying practices for your use in projects.

Chapters 5 and 6 of this book tell why Scrum works. The purpose of these chapters is to put an end to the ungrounded and contentious discussion regarding how best to build systems. Industrial process control theory is a proven body of knowledge that describes why Scrum works and other approaches are difficult and finally untenable. These chapters describe what process control theory has to say about systems development, and how Scrum arose from this discipline and theory. These chapters also lay out a terminology and framework from which empirical and adaptive approaches to systems development can ascend and flourish.

Scrum [Takeuchi and Nonaka], is a term that describes a type of product development process initially used in Japan. First used to describe hyper-productive development in 1987 by Ikujiro Nonaka and Hirotaka Takeuchi, Scrum refers to the strategy used in rugby for getting an out-of-play ball back into play. The name Scrum stuck because of the similarities between the game of rugby and the type of product development proscribed by Scrum. Both are adaptive, quick, self-organizing, and have few rests.

Building systems is hard and getting harder. Many projects are cancelled and more fail to deliver expected business value. Statistically, the information technology industry hasn't improved much despite efforts to make it more reliable and predictable. Several studies have found that about two-thirds of all projects substantially overrun their estimates [McConnell].

We find the complexity and urgency of requirements coupled with the rawness and instability of technology to be daunting. Highly motivated teams of highly skilled developers sometimes succeed, but where do you find them? If you are looking for a quick, direct way to resuscitate a troubled project, or if you are looking for a cost-effective way to succeed with new projects, try Scrum. Scrum can be started on just one project and will dramatically improve the project's probability of success.

Scrum is a management and control process that cuts through complexity to focus on building software that meets business needs. Scrum is superimposed on top of and wraps existing engineering practices, development methodologies, or standards. Scrum has been used to wrap Extreme Programming. Management and teams are able to get their hands around the requirements and technologies, never let go, and deliver working software. Scrum starts producing working functionality within one month.

Scrum deals primarily at the level of the team. It enables people to work together effectively, and by doing so, it enables them to produce complex, sophisticated products. Scrum is a kind of social engineering aiming to achieve the fulfillment of all involved by fostering cooperation. Cooperation emerges as teams self-organize in incubators nurtured by management. Using Scrum, teams develop products incrementally and empirically. Teams are guided by their knowledge and experience, rather than by formally defined project plans. In almost every instance in which Scrum has been applied, exponential productivity gains have been realized.

As authors of Scrum, we have evolved and used Scrum as an effective alternative to traditional methodologies and processes. We've written this book to help you understand our thinking, share our experiences, and repeat the success within their own organizations.

In this book, we'll be using the word "I" from now on rather than "we", "Mike", or "Ken". Unless otherwise identified, "I" will hereafter refer to Mike Beedle in chapters 6 and 7, and to Ken Schwaber elsewhere.

1.1 Scrum At Work

The best way to begin to understand Scrum is to see it at work. After using Scrum to build commercial software products, I used Scrum to help other organizations build systems. The first organization where Scrum was tested and refined was Individual, Inc. in 1996.

Individual, Inc. was in trouble and its leaders hoped that Scrum could help them out. Individual, Inc. published an online news service called NewsPage. NewsPage was initially built using proprietary technology and was subsequently licensed to companies. With the advent of the Internet, Individual, Inc. began publishing Personal NewsPage as a website for individuals.

Eight highly skilled engineers constituted the Personal NewsPage (PNP) product development team. Though the team was among the best I've worked with, it suffered from a poor reputation within Individual, Inc. It was said the PNP team couldn't produce anything, that it was a "total disaster." This belief stemmed from the fact that there hadn't been a new PNP release in nearly nine months. This was in 1996, when Internet time hadn't yet taken hold of the industry, but nine months was already far too long. When I discussed this situation with marketing, product management, and sales, they said they couldn't understand the problem. They would tell the PNP team what they wanted in no uncertain terms, but the functionality and features they requested never were delivered. When I discussed the situation with the disgruntled PNP team, it felt that it was never left alone to develop code. The engineers used the phrase "fire drill." The team would think about how to deliver a required piece of functionality, start working on it, and it would suddenly be yanked off onto the next hot idea. Whenever the PNP team committed to a project, it didn't have enough time to focus its attention before product management changed its mind, marketing told it to do something else, or sales got a great idea that had to be implemented immediately.

The situation was intolerable. Everyone was frustrated and at odds with each other. Competition was appearing on the horizon. I asked Rusty, the head of product management, to come up with a list of everything that people thought should be in PNP. He already had a list of his own and was reluctant to go to everyone and ask for his or her input. As he said, "If the PNP team can't even build what we're asking it to do now, why should we waste the effort to go through list building again?" However, Rusty did as I asked and compiled a comprehensive list. He also met with the PNP team to see if it knew of technology changes that needed to be made to implement the requirements. These were added to the list. He then prioritized the list. The PNP team gave development time estimates. Rusty sometimes changed priorities when it became apparent that items with major market impact didn't take much effort, or when it became apparent that items with minor market impact would take much more effort than they were worth.

I asked Rusty to change the product requirements process. People currently went straight to the PNP team to ask for new product features and functionality. I thought it could be more productive if it only had one source of work and wasn't interrupted. To implement this, Rusty suggested that people take their requests only to him. He added their requests to his list. He then reprioritized the list based on their presentation of the feature's importance, his estimate (after talking to someone on the PNP team) of how long it would take to implement, and the other work on the list. I advised Rusty to put every suggestion on the list. He never had to say "no." Instead, he only had to prioritize. There were no "bad" ideas, just ideas that probably would never get implemented. Rusty advised everyone at Individual, Inc. that the PNP team would only schedule work for PNP based on his prioritized list of work. He started calling his list the Product Backlog list.

Rusty liked the Product Backlog list. He never had to finalize requirements for a product release. Instead, he just maintained a list of what was needed in the product, based on the best information available to him at the time. The list was always current and always visible. He kept the Product Backlog list on a spreadsheet on a public server, so everyone knew what was going into the product next. Another benefit was that the PNP team wasn't interrupted as much. Individual, Inc. was a small company, where everyone knew each other. It had previously been hard to keep people from going straight to the PNP team with requests. Sometimes they would try approaching an engineering friend and asking for a favor: "Could you just sneak this one feature in, this once?" But Rusty insisted that all the engineers on the team stand firm. He became the keeper of the requirements, all listed by priority on the Product Backlog list.

I suggested that the company adopt a practice I had used previously: iterative, incremental development. I called each iteration a Sprint, and the results of the iteration were called a Product Increment. I suggested using Sprints so the PNP team would be left alone to focus on its task of building product functionality. It wouldn't be asked over and over again, "How's it going, are you ready to build the next thing? Have you implemented the last thing?" Sprints were intended to give the team control of its time and destiny. I also suggested a fixed duration for every Sprint. The PNP team asked for thirty days, which it felt would be enough time to build and test an increment of functionality. The team suggested putting each Product Increment into production on the web server at the end of every Sprint. The team was suggesting monthly Internet releases! All of my experience had been with shrink-wrapped software, where a new release had to be distributed to all customers who then had to schedule its implementation. Since PNP was an Internet product, it only needed to be updated in one place for all users to realize the benefits. Of course, if the team put up something that didn't work, all users would be immediately affected, so testing took on a new importance.

The PNP team met with Rusty to determine what to develop in the first Sprint. There was a lot of negotiation at this meeting, with much discussion about the details of the requirements and how to implement them. Some of the estimates changed as the implementation details were thought through. Some lower priority Product Backlog was included because it was essentially "free" once an area of code was opened for a higher priority backlog item. The meeting lasted all day. At the end of the meeting, the team had committed to implement a certain amount of the Product Backlog during the Sprint, and it had worked out a rough idea of the design and implementation details. Everyone knew what the PNP team was going to do for the next thirty days.

Of course, the PNP team was still approached innumerable times (even by Rusty) with requests to develop functionality that was not on the Product Backlog for the current Sprint. People who made these requests were asked to wait and to put these items in the Product Backlog. If their requests became top priority, they would be implemented in the next Sprint. Because the Sprint was only for thirty days, everyone could accept waiting until the end of the Sprint.

The PNP team worked without interruption during the Sprint, other than for product support and maintenance needs. PNP was still a little shaky because of the old quick and dirty process used to respond to "emergency" functionality requests. The existing policy was for the more junior engineers in technical support to make the fixes. However, these engineers were not familiar enough with the code to fix it. In order to solve this problem, I instituted the following policy: whoever writes code owns it forever. Although this detracted from the PNP team's ability to fully focus on the Sprint work, it quickly improved the quality of the code.

During the Sprint, the PNP team questioned me about what engineering techniques had to be used, what type of documentation was required, and what design artifacts had to be created. Eventually, after consulting technical support, we all agreed that how the team did its work was up to them. This was especially the case since each team member owned the code that he or she wrote in perpetuity. However, I did stipulate the PNP team had to produce an updated product technical illustration with each Sprint (and release) that could be used to understand the product design and code.

At the end of the Sprint, the PNP team had implemented the functionality it had committed to – and more. Since it had an opportunity to focus on its work for the first time, it had accomplished more than expected. The team was ready to present the Sprint Product Increment, the new release. Rusty had the team demonstrate it to management and some of the customers. The audience was delighted, and immediately authorized the team to put the new functionality up on the production web server. After a drought of nine months, the PNP team had produced a new release within one month. The team went on to repeat this performance again and again. Before I left, it had generated another five releases.

While the PNP team was working on its first Sprint, the rest of the organization was still asking it to do "favors." The team had a hard time turning down the requests, especially in a small company in which people were all friends. I decided to be the bad guy for the team. I instituted a quick, daily meeting where the team would report what it was doing. If I spotted anything that wasn't in the Product Backlog for that Sprint, I would talk to the team member who reported it after the meeting. I'd ask him or her who had asked them to do this additional work. I'd instruct him or her not to do the work. I'd go to the requestor and explain why their request wasn't being worked on, and then I'd go to Rusty to let him know of the violation. I ensured that the team was able to work on what had been agreed to and nothing else. I became the buffer between the team and the chaos of changing requirements and competitive pressures. I helped to protect the team so it could focus on its Sprint commitments. The role I assumed became known as the Scrum Master.

I had a hard time arranging the daily meeting because of the limited availability of conference rooms. When I found a room, I'd have to let everyone know which room and when we could use it. Inevitably, the word wouldn't get to someone, so not everyone would be present. New requests could slip through the cracks. I went to management and requested an office be set aside for the PNP team. I equipped this office for the team's design meetings and daily status meeting. These meetings became known as Daily Scrums, and they were held at the same time and place every day.

Everyone on the PNP team showed up for these meetings because they were helpful. The meetings were primarily to provide assistance to the PNP team. If it brought up anything it needed or anything that was getting in its way, I'd do whatever I could to remove the impediments. Once everyone on the PNP team realized this, they started to bring up other things that were getting in their way that they thought I might be able to help them with. Suddenly, a management representative was available at least once a day to help the team.

The PNP team and I got together every day for our Daily Scrum. I had scheduled 15 minutes for the meeting, but I had a hard time at first meeting the deadline. When someone reported what he or she had done, others would ask about the design. The whole team would then discuss the design, helping optimize it. Philosophical debates about best engineering practices broke out. When a decision had to be made, the whole team would try to help make it. When everyone else at Individual, Inc. found out about these meetings, they started to come. They would ask questions, offer suggestions, and generally slow everything down. Even though these visitors were well intentioned, the focus of the team was being diffused by comments and suggestions. The meeting was turning into a chaotic free-for-all, and its benefits were decreasing by the day.

Because of everything that happened during the meeting, I was unable to estimate the duration of the Daily Scrum ahead of time. Worse, the whole team had to stay through the duration of the Daily Scrum to listen. Scrum had been brought in to increase the team's productivity, but the Daily Scrum was starting to turn into a massive waste of the team's time. I instituted some very simple practices to solve this problem and return the Daily Scrum to its initial intent. First, only the team members were allowed to talk. No one else could talk. If you weren't on the team and you wanted to attend, you had to stay quiet. Second, the team was only allowed to talk about three things – what it had done since the last meeting, what it was planning on doing before the next meeting, and what was impeding its work. I called on the team members to report by going clockwise around the circle until everyone had reported.

As I ran the daily Scrums for the PNP team, it became apparent that I was fulfilling a management job. I blocked interference, allowed the team to keep focused, removed impediments and helped the team reach decisions quickly. This was a radical change, a flip, to what management had previously done. The team figured out how to do what it had committed to do. Management's new and primary job was to maximize the team's productivity, to be there to help it do the best that it could.

When I left Individual Inc., Scrum had been implemented in all three major product lines. At that time, Individual, Inc. went through a complete change in management, removing the founder and bringing in new people. Because of Scrum, though, the teams stayed focused and continued to regularly crank out new releases.

1.2   Quick Tour of Scrum

After Individual, Inc. I had a set of nomenclature and practices for Scrum. Let's take a quick tour of this Scrum. Figure 1.1 shows the overview of the Scrum process.

Scrum is often used when a systems development project is being initiated. List all of the things that the system should include and address, including functionality, features, and technology. This list is called the **Product Backlog.** The Product Backlog is a prioritized list of all product requirements. Product backlog is never finalized. Rather, it emerges and evolves along with the product. Items that have high priority on the Product Backlog are the ones that are the most desired. Product backlog content can come from anywhere: users, customers, sales, marketing, customer service, and engineering can all submit items to the backlog. However, only the **Product Owner** can prioritize the backlog. The Product Owner effectively decides the order in which things are built.

Small, cross-functional teams perform all development (**Scrum Teams**). These teams take on as much Product Backlog as they think they can turn into an increment of product functionality within a thirty-day iteration, or **Sprint**. Every Sprint must finish by delivering new executable

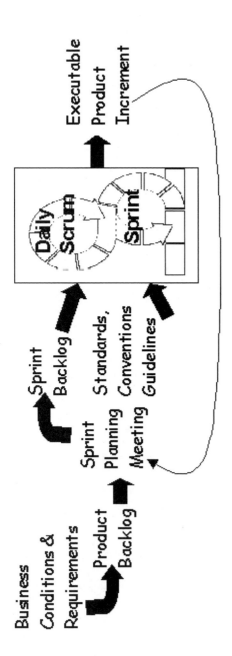

FIGURE 1.1: Scrum Summary

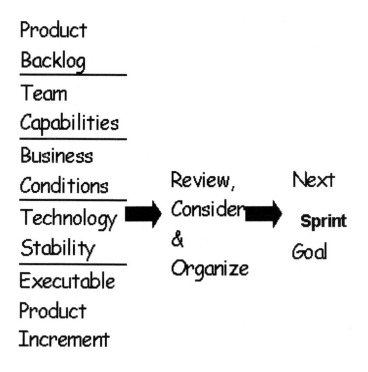

FIGURE 1.2: Input for new Sprint

product functionality. Architecture and design emerge across multiple Sprints, rather than being developed completely during the first Sprints. See Figure 1.2 Input for new Sprint for an overview of how a new Sprint is formed.

Multiple teams can develop product increments in parallel, all teams working from the same Product Backlog. The Scrum Teams are self-organizing and fully autonomous. They are constrained only by the organization's standards and conventions, and by the Product Backlog that they have selected. How the Product Backlog will be turned into a product increment is up to the team to decide. The team maintains a list of tasks to perform during each Sprint that is called a **Sprint Backlog**.

Scrum relies on team initiative and integrity. During the Sprint, a management representative (**Scrum Master**) enforces Scrum practices and helps the team to make decisions or acquire resources as needed. The team must not be disturbed or given direction by anyone outside of it while it is in a Sprint.

The Scrum Team meets daily for a short status meeting, called the **Daily Scrum**. At the Daily Scrum, progress is reviewed and impediments identified for removal by management. The Daily Scrum is an excellent place to observe how much progress a team is making.

At the end of the Sprint, the team gets together with management at a **Sprint Review Meeting** to inspect the product increment the team has built. They either build on what was developed, scavenge it, or throw it away. However, the pressure to build on what's been developed is high. The thirty day Sprint duration ensures that the worst that happens is that thirty days are lost should the team prove unable to develop any useful product functionality.

After the product increment is inspected, management often rearranges the Product Backlog to take advantage of what the team has accomplished. The Product Backlog has more meaning when viewed in light of the partially developed product. Sometimes so much product is built that management selects an earlier release schedule. In this case, the next Sprint can be used to release the product.

Once the Product Backlog has been stabilized, the team again selects top priority Product Backlog for the next Sprint. The team then goes through another iteration of work, pushing through another Sprint. This cycle continues until the product – based on **Empirically Managing** cost, time, functionality, and quality – is deemed potentially releasable. Release Sprints are then devised to bring the product to release-readiness.

Scrum is straightforward. By stripping away inappropriate and cumbersome management practices, Scrum leaves only the essence of work. Scrum leaves a team free to go to it, to work its heart out and build the best products possible. Although the Scrum process seems simple and skeletal, it provides all the necessary management and controls to focus developers and quickly build quality products.

1.3   Statements About Scrum

"The problem for engineers is that change translates into chaos, especially when a single error can potentially bring down an entire system. But, change also translates into opportunity. It's as simple as this: if there is time to put a certain amount of functionality into the product easily, then there is time to put in more functionality at the price of a certain amount of disruption and risk. Thus does madness creep into our projects - we will tend to take on as much risk as we possibly can."

James Bach. (Courtesy of Cutter Information Corp.)

1.3.1   From Jeff Sutherland

Jeff invented many of the initial thoughts and practices for Scrum prior to formalizing and commercializing Scrum with Ken Schwaber. This is a retrospective on Scrum and its implementation in five companies. —

Scrum was started for software teams at Easel Corporation in 1994 where I was VP of Object Technology. We built the first object-oriented design and analysis tool that incorporated round-trip engineering in the initial Scrum-based project. A second Scrum-based project implemented the first product to completely automate object-relational mapping in an enterprise development environment. I was assisted by two world-class developers, Jeff McKenna, now an Extreme Programming (XP) consultant, and John Scumniotales, now a development leader for object-oriented design tools at Rational Corporation.

In 1995, Easel was acquired by VMARK, and Scrum continued there until I joined Individual in 1996 as VP of Engineering. I asked Ken Schwaber to help me incorporate Scrum into Individual's development process. In the same year I took Scrum to IDX when I assumed the positions of Senior VP of Engineering and Product Development and CTO. IDX, one of the largest healthcare software companies, was the proving ground for multiple-team Scrum implementations. At one point, I had over 600 developers workings on dozens of products. In 2000, I introduced Scrum to PatientKeeper, a mobile/wireless healthcare platform company where I became CTO. So I have experienced Scrum in five companies, with consulting assistance from Ken Schwaber in three of those companies. These companies varied widely in size and were proving grounds for Scrum in all phases of company growth: from startup, to initial IPO, to mid-size, and then to large company with a 30-year track record.

There were some key factors that influenced the introduction of Scrum at Easel Corporation. The book *Wicked Problems, Righteous Solutions* [DeGrace] reviewed the reasons why the waterfall approach to software development does not work today. Requirements are not fully understood before the project begins. The user knows what they want only after they see an initial version of the software. Requirements change during the software construction process. New tools and technologies make implementation strategies unpredictable. DeGrace and Stahl reviewed "All-at-Once" models of software development that uniquely fit object-oriented implementation of software.

The team–based "All-at-Once" model was based on the Japanese approach to new product development, Sashimi and Scrum. We were already using production prototyping to build software. It was implemented in slices (Sashimi) where an entire piece of fully integrated functionality worked at the end of an iteration. What intrigued us was Takeuchi and Nonaka's description of the team building process in setting up and managing a Scrum [Takeuchi and Nonaka]. The idea of building a self-empowered team where everyone had the global view of the product being built seemed like the right idea. The approach to managing the team that had been so successful at Honda, Canon, and Fujitsu resonated with the systems thinking approach being promoted by Senge at MIT [Senge].

We were also impacted by recent publications in computer science. Peter Wegner at Brown University demonstrated that it was impossible to fully specify or test an interactive system designed to respond to external inputs, i.e. Wegner's Lemma [Wegner]. Here was mathematical proof that any process that assumed known inputs, like the waterfall method, was doomed to failure when building an object-oriented system. We were prodded into setting up the first Scrum meeting after reading Coplien's paper on Borland's development of Quattro Pro for Windows. The Quattro team delivered one million lines of C++ code in 31 months with a 4 person staff growing to 8 people later in the project. This was about 1000 lines of deliverable code per person per week, probably the most productive project ever documented. The team attained this level of productivity by intensive interaction in daily meetings with project management, product management, developers, documenters, and quality assurance staff.

Our daily meetings which we started at Easel were disciplined in the way we now understand as the Scrum pattern [ScrumPattern]. The most interesting effect in a Smalltalk development environment was "punctuated equilibrium". A fully integrated component design environment leads to rapid evolution of a software system with emergent, adaptive properties resembling the process of punctuated equilibrium observed in biological species.

It is well understood in biological evolution that change occurs sharply at intervals separated by long periods of apparent stagnation, leading to the concept of punctuated equilibrium [Dennett]. Computer simulations of this phenomenon suggest that periods of equilibrium are actually periods of ongoing genetic change of an organism. The effects of that change are not apparent until several subsystems evolve in parallel to the point where they can work together to produce a dramatic external effect [Levy]. This punctuated equilibrium effect has been observed by teams working in a component based environment with adequate business process engineering tools, and the Scrum development process accentuates the effect.

By having every member of the team see every day what every other team member was doing, we began to get comments from one developer that if he changed a few lines of code, he could eliminate days of work for another developer. This effect was so dramatic that the project accelerated to the point where **it had to be slowed down.** This hyper productive state was seen in several subsequent Scrums but never so dramatically as the one at Easel. It was a combination of the skill of the team, the flexibility of Smalltalk, and way we approached production prototypes that evolved into deliverable product.

A project domain can be viewed as a set of packages that will form a release. Packages are what the user perceives as pieces of functionality and they evolve out of work on topic areas. Topic areas are business object

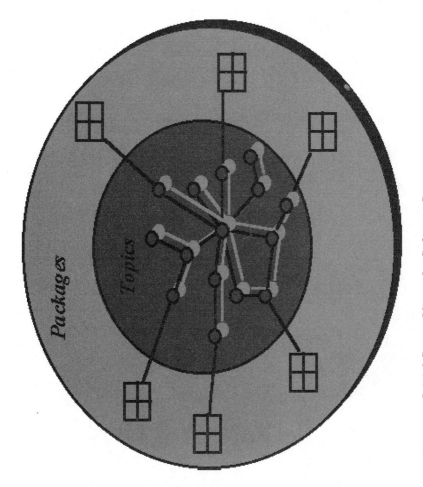

FIGURE 1.3: Initial Scrum View of a Software System

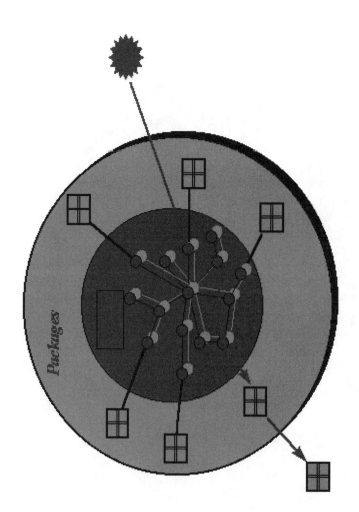

FIGURE 1.4: Firing a Synchstep

components. Changes are introduced into the system by introducing a unit of work that alters a component. The unit of work in the initial Scrum was called a Synchstep.

System evolution proceeds in Synchsteps. After one or more Synchsteps have gone to completion and forced some refactoring throughout the system, or often simply provided new functionality to existing components, a new package of functionality emerges that is observable to the user. These Synchsteps are similar to genetic mutations. Typically, several interrelated components must mutate in concert to produce a significant new piece of functionality. And this new functionality appears as a "punctuated equilibrium" effect to builders of the system. For a period of time the system is stable with no new behavior. Then when a certain (somewhat unpredictable) Synchstep completes, the whole system pops up to a new level of functionality, often surprising the development team.

The key to entering a hyper productive state was not just the Scrum organizational pattern. We did constant component testing of topic areas, integration of packages, and refactoring of selected parts of the system. These activities have become key features of XP [Fowler].

Furthermore, in the hyper productive state, the initial Scrum entered the "zone". No matter what happened or what problems arose, the response of the team always was far better than the response of any individual. It reminded me of the stories about the Celtics basketball team at their peak, where they could do no wrong. The impact of entering the "zone" was not just hyper productivity. The personal lives of the people were changed. People said they would never forget working on such a project and they would always be looking for another experience like it. It induced open, team-oriented, fun–loving behavior in unexpected persons and eliminated those who were not productive from the team through peer embarrassment.

When Easel Corporation was acquired by VMARK (now Informix), the original Scrum team continued their work on the same product. The VMARK senior management team was intrigued by Scrum and asked me to run a senior management team Scrum once a week to drive all the companies' products to the Internet. These meetings started in 1995 and within a few months, the team had caused the introduction of two new Internet products and repositioned leading current products as Internet applications. Some members of this team left VMARK to become innovators in emerging Internet companies. So Scrum had an early impact on the Internet.

In the spring of 1996, I returned to a company I cofounded as VP of Engineering. Ken Schwaber has documented much of the Scrum experience at Individual. The most impressive thing to me about Scrum at Individual was not that the team delivered two new Internet products in a single quarter, and multiple releases of one of the products. It was the fact that Scrum eliminated about 8 hours a week of senior management meeting time starting the day the Scrum began. Because the company had just gone public at the beginning of the Internet explosion, there were multiple competing priorities and constant revision of market strategy. As a result, the development team was constantly changing priorities and unable to deliver product. And the management team was meeting almost daily to determine status of implementation of priorities that were viewed differently by every manager.

The solution was to force all decisions to occur in the daily Scrum meeting. If anyone wanted any status or wanted to influence any priority, they could only do it in the Scrum. I remember in the early phase, the SVP of Marketing sat in on every meeting for a couple of weeks sharing her desperate concern about meeting Internet deliverables and timetables. The effect on the team was not to immediate respond to her despair. Over a period of two weeks, the team self-organized around a plan to meet her priorities with achievable technical delivery dates. When she agreed to the plan, she no longer had to attend any Scrum or status meetings. The Scrum reported status on the web with green lights, yellow lights, and red lights for pieces of functionality. In this way the entire company knew status in real time, all the time.

During the summer of 1996, IDX Systems hired me away from Individual to be their SVP of Engineering and Product Development. I replaced the technical founder of the company who had led development for almost 30 years. IDX had over 4000 customers and was one of the largest healthcare software companies with hundreds of developers working on dozens of products. Here was an opportunity to extend Scrum to large-scale development.

The approach at IDX was to turn the entire development organization into an interlocking set of Scrums. Every part of the organization was team based, including the management team that included two vice presidents, a senior architect, and several directors. Front line Scrums met daily. A Scrum of Scrums that included the team leaders of each Scrum in a product line met weekly. The management Scrum met monthly.

The key learning at IDX was Scrum scales to any size. With dozens of teams in operation, the most difficult problem is ensuring the quality of the Scrum process in each team, particularly when the entire organization has to learn Scrum all at once. IDX was large enough to bring in leading productivity experts to monitor productivity on every project. While most teams were only able to meet the industry average in function points per month delivered, several teams moved into a hyper productive state producing deliverable functionality at 4-5 times the industry average. These teams became shining stars in the organization and examples for the rest of the organization to follow.

In early 2000, I joined PatientKeeper, Inc. as Chief Technology Officer and began introducing Scrum into a startup company. I was the 21st
employee and we grew the development team from a dozen people to 45
people in six months. PatientKeeper deploys mobile devices in healthcare
institutions to capture and process financial and clinical data. Server technology synchronizes the mobile devices and moves data to and from multiple backend legacy systems. A complex technical architecture provides
enterprise application integration to hospital and clinical systems. Data is
forward deployed from these systems in a PatientKeeper clinical repository.
Server technologies migrate changes from our clinical repository to a cache
and then to data storage on the mobile device. Scrum works equally well
across technology implementations. The key learning at PatientKeeper has
been around introduction of Extreme Programming (XP) techniques as a
way to implement code delivered by a Scrum organization. While all teams
seem to find it easy to implement a Scrum organizational process, they do
not always find it easy to introduce new XP programming. We have been
able to do some team programming and constant testing and refactoring,
particularly as we have migrated all development to Java and XML. It has
been more difficult to introduce these ideas when developers are working
in C and C++, our legacy technology.

After introducing Scrum into five different companies with different
sizes and different technologies, I can confidently say that Scrum works in
any environment and can scale into programming in the large. In all cases,
it will radically improve communication and delivery of working code. The
next challenge for Scrum, in my view, is to provide a tight integration of the
Scrum organization pattern and XP programming techniques. I believe this
integration can generate more hyper productive Scrums on a predictable
basis. The first Scrum did this intuitively before XP was born and that was
its key to extreme performance and life changing experience. In addition,
the participation of Scrum leaders in the Agile Alliance [Agile], which has
absorbed all leaders of well-known lightweight development processes, will
facilitate wider use of Scrum and its integration with extreme programming.

1.3.2   From Ken Schwaber

**Ken developed and formalized the Scrum process for systems
development.**   —

My company, Advanced Development Methods (ADM), built and sold
process management software in the early 1990's. Many IT organizations
used ADM's product, MATE (Methods and Tool Expert), to automate
their methodologies. For example, Coopers & Lybrand used MATE to automate SUMMIT D^{TM}, their systems development methodology, for both

internal use and use by their customers. IBM also used MATE, automating its outsourcing, software development, and change management methodologies with it. The methodologies that MATE automated for these companies were the traditional "heavy" methodologies.

In MATE's heyday, the backlog of development work was daunting. Coopers & Lybrand and IBM were using MATE extensively, as were many of their customers. The number of requests for new functionality, new interfaces, and "nice-to-haves" was quite large. It was chaos! To help make sense of everything, I built a Product Backlog list; here I listed all requested functionality, planned technology, planned enhancements, and major bugs. I worked with our customers, including Coopers & Lybrand and IBM, to prioritize the list. However, the priorities never stayed still. They were always changing based on the most recent input from a customer or potential customer.

When I looked at everything ADM had to do, I was overwhelmed. I figured the next release was probably a year away. I realized that even if ADM achieved everything on Product Backlog, no one would be satisfied since requirements would have changed by the release date. In desperation, I started identifying product functionality that could be built in monthly cycles. At the end of the month, I'd review what had been built with the customers to see if I was on track. To my surprise, the customers were delighted with this approach. When they saw what ADM had built, they often changed their minds regarding their priorities. They often wanted to take immediate advantage of what was at hand, maybe with a few more tweaks.

I changed ADM's development process to use two sequential cycles of one month each. In the first cycle, ADM would build functionality. In the second cycle, ADM would prepare it for release. If any engineers had extra time during the release cycle, they'd work on adding more to the next release cycle. The two-cycle approach seemed simple enough, but it had ramifications on the development and release environments. ADM really had to have the code management and release management systems and procedures thoroughly in place for this to work. Daily builds became a necessity. The rapid release cycle forced me to significantly upgrade all of the engineering practices. As a result, ADM became very efficient.

ADM built MATE using object-oriented technology (OO). In 1993, Jeff Sutherland, an active member in the Object Management Group (OMG) and the various OOPSLA SIG's (and a good friend) asked what methodology was used by ADM. Jeff was sure that ADM was using one of its client's methodologies. I still remember the look on Jeff's face when I told him, "None – if ADM used any of them, it would be out of business."

Jeff wanted to know what methodology ADM used because he was impressed by the short duration of ADM's development cycles and the frequent releases of MATE. He wanted to understand so he could make OO similarly productive. At that time, OO wasn't delivering the productivity that its proponents had initially promised and criticism was mounting.

Jeff had been head of engineering and development at Easel and then VMARK (both major software product vendors) and had long used and advocated OO. Jeff had also read about a new product development philosophy called Scrum. Jeff had implemented his interpretation of it at both Easel and VMARK. He hoped that my experience with the major methodologies would help him further formulate Scrum.

That conversation with Jeff was the beginning of a joint effort to formalize Scrum. We read everything that we could get our hands on, sometimes surprising ourselves when other fields such as complexity theory added to our understanding. We saw corollaries in chaos and complexity theory, recognized the beauty of emergent processes, and gained a better understanding of self-organization. We were profoundly influenced by research regarding software development practices at Borland and Microsoft. Of particular influence was their fierce focus on code. The final research occurred at DuPont's Experimental Station in Wilmington, Delaware, where experts in process control theory reviewed our work and provided the theoretical foundations for Scrum.

Jeff and I worked together to create a formal description of the Scrum process. Scrum went from being a collection of thoughts that Jeff and I posted on our websites to a development methodology that I presented at OOPSLA'96. Since then, Scrum has become a major alternative to classic product development approaches. It has been adopted both by managers who wanted to ensure they got the best product they could, and by engineers who wanted to ensure they would be able to do their best work. Since its introduction, Scrum has been used in thousands of projects worldwide. Mike, Jeff and I have personally implemented Scrum in hundreds of projects, and we've worked with and advised others in the United States, Europe, Australia, New Zealand, Singapore, the Philippines, Hong Kong, Ethiopia, and Indonesia. Scrum has been implemented for single projects as well as an organizational product development process. Scrum has been used for such diverse, complex efforts as readying a product and customer base for a new Y2K compliant release, preparing a tunable laser subsystem for fiber optic networks for a trade show, and rapidly creating advanced teleradiology systems.

1.3.3   From Mike Beedle

Mike has long been a Scrum innovator and practitioner. Mike recently has wrapped Extreme Programming engineering practices with Scrum.   —

I am the president and founder of e-Architects Inc., a software development consulting company in Chicago specializing in distributed objects and Internet technologies.

I started practicing Scrum *explicitly* in the fall of 1995, when I saved a company's division from going bankrupt. I had the good fortune to read a message from Jeff Sutherland and to recognize that this was in fact *very* important information. He announced that he and Ken Schwaber were working on a method called Scrum that basically documented what people *really* did to deliver systems. I was fascinated with the information provided at their websites and I immediately adopted the practices in a project I was running in Chicago. The project was successful and the rest is history: I became a Scrum convert and Scrum practitioner for life. To read the whole story please see Chapter 7: Advanced Scrum Applications, Case Study of Large Project: An Outsourcing Company.

Since then, however, I have used Scrum in almost every project I have been involved with for the last 6 years and I have introduced Scrum to many companies: William M. Mercer, Nike Securities, Motorola, Northwest Bank, Lincoln Reinsurance, AllState Insurance, and Caremark. With Scrum, e-Architects has developed many applications in a wide-range of domains and environments, and it has always contributed significantly to simplify and accelerate software development. For the last year, we have also wrapped XP with Scrum with superb results: XP enhances the quality of the software developed and Scrum enhances the day-to-day management of the projects. I call this union of Scrum and XP XBreed, which stands for "crossbreed". Find more information on this at: www.xbreed.net.

I have been involved in professional software development for the last 23 years. And since then, I have seen many kinds of software development: 1) big five methods like Andersen's Method/1, 2) varied software vendors' methods like IBM's and Microsoft's software development methods, 3) mission-critical methods like Texas Instruments, MCI, Sprint, Goldman Sachs, 4) CMM government contractors like Motorola, General Dynamics, 5) methods given by methodologists like De Marco's, Yourdon's, Booch's, Rumbaugh's, Schlaer-Mellor's, Jacobson's, including the later unified process frameworks like RUP© (Rational Unified Process™); and even several kinds of 6) hacking, *a la* novice programmer and *a la* MIT's 60's style.

I definitely haven't seen all styles of software development, but I have seen enough to say – though this may sound strange – that *despite the method used, most everyone that delivers software to production eventually starts doing something very similar to Scrum.* In other words, the Scrum practices are hidden but simple universal *patterns* that have been forgotten by most of us. In fact, another way we have looked at Scrum in the last few years is just as collection of organizational patterns [ScrumPattern].

As an experiment, do this: take three programmers and give them a project and a room. To begin the project, they will talk to the customer and find out what the customer wants and what is important to him or her. Together with the customer they will create a prioritized "feature list" – in Scrum we call this a Product Backlog. To actually implement something, they will meet with the customer and choose some features to implement first based on the priority of the features – in Scrum we call the meeting a Sprint Planning Meeting and the list of items to be implemented the Sprint Backlog. As they develop the software, they will run into issues and add them to their iteration "to do" list (i.e. their Sprint Backlog). To see where everyone is, they will have informal meetings to tell each other what they are working on, what issues they have and what they will be working on next – in Scrum we call these meetings Daily Scrums. As they implement features they will show their management and their customer how things look – in Scrum we call this Sprint Review Meeting.

However, if managing a software project is so simple, why do we have thousands of volumes of project management without this information? If these activities are so natural and common sense, why is this knowledge not explicit? If these activities are taking place despite the method used when deliveries to production take place, why are they not documented? If these are the steps that really drive a project, why do we waste our time with other things?

This is why I am writing this book. This information is first and foremost, important, but it is also the most *natural, simple, and common sense* way to manage a software project. Somewhere along the line, we forgot this basic and instinctive way of managing software projects, but unfortunately, we pay a very high price for this memory loss.

I cordially invite you to try Scrum. You won't regret it.

1.4 How the Book Is Organized

Chapters 2, 3, and 4 are for the reader that wants to understand Scrum and apply it to a project or organization.

Chapter 2 (*Get Ready for Scrum!*) provides an overview of how Scrum is different, why it works, and what it feels like in a Scrum project.

Chapter 3 (*Scrum Practices*) is a step-by-step description of how Scrum works. Follow the instructions in this chapter and you'll be using Scrum.

Chapter 4 (*Applying Scrum*) defines management principles and practices for building products and systems with Scrum. Iterative, incremental systems development requires empirical management practices. This chapter shows how to use these practices.

Chapters 5 and 6 provide the theoretical underpinnings for Scrum and other similar system and product development practices. These chapters are for the advanced reader.

Chapter 5 (Why Scrum?) lays the theoretical foundations for Scrum as an empirical process control mechanism for systems and product development. Described within the context of universal "noise", this chapter lays out why, in theory and practice, the empirical approach works and the defined approach doesn't work. This chapter provides the basis for overturning inappropriate application of defined processes to systems development projects.

Chapter 6 (*Why Does Scrum Work?*) includes some interesting ways to look at Scrum. These perspectives can help you understand how and why Scrum works. These perspectives offer us, the authors, points for more research and definition into the Scrum process.

Chapters 7, 8, and 9 provide additional information that is useful for the readers that have proceeded past the initial Scrum project.

Chapter 7 (*Advanced Scrum Applications*) provides some guidance for those who want to apply Scrum in different kinds of circumstances. Particular attention is paid to reuse and large projects.

Chapter 8 (*Scrum and the Organization*) discusses the impact that Scrum can have on an organization as impediments are removed and the organization adjusts itself to high productivity development.

Chapter 9 (*Scrum Values*) describes the values that emerge when an organization uses Scrum.

CHAPTER 2

Get Ready For Scrum!

Scrum is different. Work feels different. Management feels different. Under Scrum, work becomes straightforward, relevant, and productive. —

2.1 Scrum Is Different

I've spent a good part of my professional life building technology products and systems. I've had successes, and I've certainly had failures. I think I'm not alone when I say that most systems development projects are difficult. I suspect also that they are harder than they need to be. I remember a project when I worked with a plant manager at a pharmaceutical company. Together, he and I implemented a complicated material requirements planning system. As we were about to successfully complete the project, I congratulated him and told him that he could make a lot of money helping other companies implement similar systems. He looked at me aghast, and said, "I'll never go through something this gruesome again. I can't wait to go back to just managing the business!" His observation was one of many that led me to think that something was wrong; there must be a more straightforward way to build and implement systems.

Every project is different. The technology, the requirements, and the people are different every time. I've studied a variety of approaches to project management in an effort to make my life easier and the teams more productive despite their differences. I've tried new development environments, modeling tools, technologies, methodologies, people approaches, everything and anything to improve the process of building a system. I've found some things that improved my life, like always using the best engineers, forming cross-functional teams, and facilitating design sessions around white boards. These tactics all help, but without Scrum these projects were all eventually overwhelmed by the complexity inherent in systems development projects.

I once placed my hopes on commercially available methodologies. They contain templates of work that have previously been used to build systems. They therefore contain tried and true processes that other professionals have successfully used. Companies that build software for a living usually sell methodologies. I always assumed that for this very reason, the methodologies must be really good.

Methodologies are like cookbooks: follow their recipes and a successful system will result. Some methodologies are modest in scope and depth, while others contain literally thousands of pieces of work, or tasks, tied together into templates. Each template is appropriate for a specific type of development project.

Over the years I used commercial methodologies, they added definition to my projects. I knew what to do, when to do it, and I could assign people to the work. I felt like I was more in control and each project had a lot to show for it. Unfortunately, my success rate did not increase. One company that I worked at cancelled a major project after two years. I toured the project space not long after its cancellation and found a ghost town. There were hundreds of cubicles full of workstations and books of standards, training materials, requirements manuals, and design documents. Unfortunately, this project hadn't been successful. The project never even reached the software construction phase of the project, so no functionality was ever delivered.

As I mentioned earlier, I ran a software company in the early 1990's that developed and licensed a process management product called MATE. Our largest customers were Coopers & Lybrand and IBM, and they wanted us to employ their methodologies to build MATE. I attempted it and was thoroughly displeased with the results. At the time, my company's requirements were always changing and we were working with new technologies. It looked like the methodologies should help, but instead they just got in our way, decreased our flexibility, and generally slowed us down.

I wanted to understand the reason why my customers' methodologies didn't work for my company, so I brought several systems development methodologies to process theory experts at the DuPont Experimental Station in 1995. These experts, led by Babatunde "Tunde" Ogannaike, are the most highly respected theorists in industrial process control. They know process control inside and out. Some of them even taught the subject at major universities. They had all been brought in by DuPont to automate the entire product flow, from forecasts and orders to product delivery.

They inspected the systems development processes that I brought them. I have rarely provided a group with so much laughter. They were amazed and appalled that my industry, systems development, was trying to do its work using a completely inappropriate process control model. They said systems development had so much complexity and unpredictability that it had to be managed by a process control model they referred to as "empirical." They said this was nothing new, and all complex processes that weren't completely understood required the empirical model. They helped me go through a book that is the Bible of industrial process control theory, *Process Dynamics, Modeling and Control* [Tunde] to understand why I was off track.

In a nutshell, there are two major approaches to controlling any process. The "defined" process control model requires that every piece of work be completely understood. Given a well-defined set of inputs, the same outputs are generated every time. A defined process can be started and allowed to run until completion, with the same results every time. Tunde said the methodologies that I showed him attempted to use the defined model, but none of the processes or tasks were defined in enough detail to provide repeatability and predictability. Tunde said my business was an intellectually intensive business that required too much thinking and creativity to be a good candidate for the defined approach. He theorized that my industry's application of the defined methodologies must have resulted in a lot of surprises, loss of control, and incomplete or just wrong products. He was particularly amused that the tasks were linked together with dependencies, as though they could predictably start and finish just like a well defined industrial process.

Tunde told me the empirical model of process control, on the other hand, expects the unexpected. It provides and exercises control through frequent inspection and adaptation for processes that are imperfectly defined and generate unpredictable and unrepeatable outputs. He recommended I study this model and consider its application to the process of building systems.

During my visit to DuPont, I experienced a true epiphany. Suddenly, something in me clicked and I realized why everyone in my industry had such problems building systems. I realized why the industry was in such trouble and had such a poor reputation. We were wasting our time trying to control our work by thinking we had an assembly line when the only proper control was frequent and first-hand inspection, followed by immediate adjustments.

Based on this insight, I have since formulated with others the Scrum process for developing complex products, particularly software systems. Scrum is based on the empirical process control model. For those interested, more details on why Scrum works are presented in Chapter 5: *Why Scrum?* and Chapter 6: *Why Does Scrum Work?*

Scrum is a way of doing things that is completely different from what most people in the software and product development industry are used to. All of the assumptions, mechanisms, and ways of looking at things are so different that a new way of thinking evolves as you begin to use Scrum. Scrum feels and looks different because it is based on the empiricism. Less time is spent trying to plan and define tasks, and less time is spent creating and reading management reports. More time is spent with the project team understanding what is happening and empirically responding. Most people really understand Scrum only when they begin to use it. A light bulb goes off when they experience its simplicity and productivity. They realize how inappropriate more traditional models of development process are for our industry.

The following case study covers an implementation of Scrum and the application of empiricism. In it, I describe working closely with a team to build a product while using the Scrum process. In this example, I made decisions and encouraged the team to act differently than they were used to acting. I taught them by example to approach their work in an entirely different way. By the time we had completed the first Sprint, the team was already behaving differently. They had seen Scrum work, and now they were Scrum users. They had come to embody the values integral to Scrum, such as empiricism, self-organization, and action.

As you read the case study, think about what is missing from it. There is no formal project planning phase. There aren't any Pert charts. There are no roles and individual assignments. Notice how the team is able to get on with its work and build valuable product increments anyway. Notice the team self-organize from a dispirited group of individuals waiting for instructions into a team that takes the initiative and acts. By the end of the first Sprint, the team had adopted a completely new set of values and begun to act unlike any other team at the organization.

2.2   A Noisy Project

The project was to build a middleware business object server and its accompanying business objects. A large financial institution wanted to develop the product to connect its online transactions to its legacy databases. The institution needed to handle increasing transaction volumes, to standardize database access, and to carry out the implementation of new technologies such as telephone, wireless, and handheld input devices. This technology was all devastatingly complicated, including choices and learning curves for object technology, transaction management, hardware, operating systems, and development environments. To complicate matters, this was a technically sophisticated company, so proponents for various alternatives to each technology choice were numerous and vociferous. Furthermore, team members were working at multiple locations, and the team therefore needed to use a multi-site development environment technology. It had chosen to use an enterprise-wide code management software, but had not yet begun to do so.

The project was truly hellish. A development team had been chartered and charged. When I first began working with the team, it had been in existence for four months, but had not built any product. It was waiting for a budget. It was waiting for funding for new servers, for the last team members to be assigned, for the code management software to be licensed, and for someone who knew how to administer the code management software to be hired.

To begin implementing Scrum, I started holding Daily Scrum meetings. These meetings are supposed to be quick status updates. This was not the case at the first Daily Scrums. The first meeting took three hours, rather than the customary fifteen minutes. Everyone was completely dispirited and demoralized. Team members talked not about what they were doing, but about what was preventing them from doing anything. Many people complained that management didn't support the project, and everyone was upset the budget hadn't been formalized. Without a budget, the team couldn't order servers or license the code management software. For that matter, the team couldn't attract new team members, since it looked as though it was going nowhere fast. The team was without funding, without a sponsor, and without the tools that it needed.

2.3   Cut Through the Noise By Taking Action

One of the fundamental principles of Scrum is "the art of the possible." That is, Scrum instructs teams not to dwell on what can't be done, but to think about what can be done. Teams are put in a time box and told to create product. It is important to focus on what can be done and how the problem can be solved with the available resources. This team had a name, a scope, and definition, and it was staffed with some really solid engineers, all of whom had workstations and access to a lot of software. I asked the team what it could do with the available resources. I also asked the team whether it believed that the problem it was trying to solve was important to the organization.

The team confirmed that the problem was real and it was eager to tackle it. Some team members were aware that a customer service project was being held up by the very problem they were supposed to solve. The customer service project was supposed to implement access to the legacy databases, but was unable to proceed because this team had not yet built the middleware server that would handle legacy database access. Clearly, this team had been chartered because of a critical organizational need, and it had an important mission to accomplish. Until the team could get moving, other projects would continue to be held up.

The team quickly identified a core set of transactions that the customer service project needed it to enable. The team members felt that they had enough skills to build a middleware object server to implement these transactions, so long as someone from the customer service team worked with them as a domain expert. They felt they knew AIX, Tuxedo, and CORBA well enough to use that technology to implement the solution. They "borrowed" an RS6000 server from the server room to develop and prototype their work. The project manager, Herb, presented this plan of attack to his management. Since this effort required no additional funding and no administrative action, Herb was authorized to proceed. I got together with the team and devised a goal for the first Sprint. The Sprint goal was:

Sprint Goal: to provide a standardized middleware mechanism for the identified customer service transactions to access backend databases.

The team figured out the work they would have to do to meet the Sprint goal. The following tasks came up:

Map the transaction elements to backend database tables.

Write a business object in C++ to handle transactions via defined methods and interfaces.

Wrap the C++ in a CORBA wrapper.

Use Tuxedo for all queuing, messaging, and transaction management.

Measure the transaction performance to determine whether scalability requirements can be met.

2.4   Self-Organization

After identifying these objectives, the team began the Sprint. Since the team was using familiar technology, there were no major technological problems. However, two team members were at a remote site. Because the team didn't have an enterprise-wide code management system, it couldn't readily do multi-site code management. This problem was resolved by partitioning responsibilities between the two sites, and verbally coordinating whenever either site had to use code under the other's control.

The team met and decided who would do what work. When one team member wanted to work with the Tuxedo expert to learn the product, the team figured out how the rest of the team could pick up the slack. As the team started doing the work, it would meet frequently on its own to design the product and further identify and parse the work. The team did this on its own. It knew the Sprint Goal and its commitment. The team was figuring out how to live up to its commitment.

2.5   Respond Empirically

After ten days, the team started to feel like it was going to fail. The technology was up and working, it had figured out the CORBA wrapper, and it had accessed the appropriate databases. However, the team felt that it couldn't get the entire selected customer service transaction set mapped and linked to the database within the Sprint. The transaction data was too complicated and involved too many tables and indices for the mapping to be completed in thirty days.

The team had incorrectly anticipated the complexity and the scope of the work it had assigned to itself. But had it failed? Not in the eyes of Scrum. Working with a host of difficult technologies and unknown transactions, the team had built the development environment, put up a middleware server using Tuxedo, and had started implementing the customer service transactions. It was doing great. The team had done the best that it could rather than sitting around and doing nothing.

Again, I focused the team on the art of the possible. What could it do within the Sprint and still meet the goal? The goal wasn't to complete the entire transaction set, even though that was what the team had expected to be able to do. The goal was to prove the viability of a middleware object server providing database access to the customer service transaction set. No one even knew whether management would approve and fund this approach. The team quickly identified that they could address a reduced scope of transaction data elements involving fewer tables and indices, and then proceeded to automate this.

2.6   Daily Visibility Into the Project

On the fourteenth day of the Sprint I held our Daily Scrum. When it came to Tom's turn to report, he indicated that a Senior-Vice President, Lou, had instructed him to build something that was not within the scope of work for the Sprint. Consequently, he had been unable to do the work that the rest of the team had expected of him, though he would try to catch up. I immediately went to Lou's office and asked what was up. Lou had been offsite and had learned that a potential customer was interested in additional functionality. He had decided to help the team out by instructing one of its members to start developing that functionality.

Lou hadn't been at all of the Scrum training, so he didn't know that interrupting a Sprint is almost always more counterproductive than it is helpful. Lou didn't know that the team was protected during the Sprint from external chaos, complexity, and uncertainty. Lou said that if he saw a $100 bill on the ground on the way to the train, he would bend over and pick it up, and that he didn't see how this situation was any different. I told Lou that, in the greater scheme of things, his family would probably appreciate his getting home on time more than the $100. I explained to Lou the importance of not disrupting a Sprint, and he agreed to refrain from doing so in the future. By the end of the Sprint, the feature that Lou had wanted to be demonstrated was no longer on the radar of this potential customer anyway. Apparently, it had only been of interest to the customer as a conversation topic with Lou at the offsite.

2.7   Incremental Product Delivery

At the end-of-Sprint demonstration, the team really impressed management with its pragmatism and empiricism. With only the resources it had on hand, it had proven that its approach was technically feasible. In fact, it had put the technology to use for customer service functionality. Although a thorough requirements study might eventually have uncovered better technical approaches, the team had used available resources to solve the problem both for the customer service team and for the company as a whole. The team had been productive with what was on hand.

The team had run performance measures on its solution and proven that the approach could handle the expected transaction volumes. In an online session, it showed management part of the transaction going through the middleware to the databases, retrieving and displaying selected data, and doing so with performance and scalability that could be sustained.

The team presented an increment of product that was successful, could be discussed, and could be built upon. If the team had not gotten its act together, the organization as a whole would have been thirty days closer to a transaction volume meltdown. Instead, because of their empiricism, effort and initiative, the organization had something that worked and that could be modified and built upon. Incremental product delivery can be very powerful, providing an organization with real progress in a short period of time. Previously, the organization was wrapped around its spokes discussing how to proceed.

The team had provided a starting point, a prototype that validated the approach and could be built upon. The team quickly gained formal status and funding, and eventually came up with a solution for legacy database access.

By using Scrum, the team was able to cut through the noise and start delivering valuable product. Time that would have otherwise been wasted was spent working. The team was able to focus itself and deliver product. Management was able to help the team stay focused. The team continued for another year, building a general-purpose middleware business object server with access to specific databases. The team members became consultants to other organizations that used the middleware. As they consulted, they spread Scrum.

In the next sections, I'll describe the details of the Scrum practices I implemented in this case study so that you, also, can implement Scrum and manage Scrum projects.

CHAPTER 3

Scrum Practices

A set of Scrum practices and rules establishes an environment within which products can be rapidly and incrementally built in complex environments. These practices have been established experientially through thousands of Scrum projects. —

In this chapter, I'll describe how to make Scrum work. I'll start by introducing the Scrum Master, the person that manages the Scrum process in an organization. Then I'll discuss setting up a project by defining the Scrum Teams and building the list of work that drives the Sprint iterations. The Daily Scrum and the End-Of-Sprint review are looked at next, and I'll describe how to inspect and respond to the unexpected. Lastly, I'll talk about the combustion chamber, the Sprint iteration, where teams grapple with complex requirements and technology to build product increments.

Scrum practices have evolved during its application to thousands of development projects. I strongly recommend these practices be strictly adhered to until you understand why and how Scrum works from experience, not just reading this book. Once Scrum is working well in your organization, once people have adopted the values that make Scrum work, then you can make adjustments. Before you start tinkering, make sure you've learned from experience. Think of Scrum like skiing. Until you've been up on skis and experienced the sensation of skiing, you can't adequately understand the impact of changes. Learn first, then make changes.

3.1 The Scrum Master

The Scrum Master is responsible for the success of Scrum. —

The Scrum Master is a new management role introduced by Scrum. The Scrum Master is responsible for ensuring that Scrum values, practices, and rules are enacted and enforced. The Scrum Master is the driving force behind all of the Scrum practices in this chapter; he or she sets them up them up and makes them happen.

The Scrum Master represents management and the team to each other. At the Daily Scrum, the Scrum Master listens closely to what each team member reports. He or she compares what progress has been made to what progress was expected, based on Sprint goals and predictions made during the previous Daily Scrum. For example, if someone has been working on a trivial task for three days, he or she probably needs help. The Scrum Master tries to gauge the velocity of the team: is it stuck, is it floundering, is it making progress? If the team needs assistance, the Scrum Master meets with it to see what he or she can do to help.

The Scrum Master works with the customers and management to identify and institute a Product Owner. The Scrum Master works with management to form Scrum teams. The Scrum Master then works with the Product Owner and the Scrum teams to create Product Backlog for a Sprint. The Scrum Master works with the Scrum teams to plan and initiate the Sprint. During the Sprint, the Scrum Master conducts all Daily Scrums, and is responsible for ensuring that impediments are promptly removed and decisions are promptly made. The Scrum Master is also responsible for working with management to gauge progress and reduce backlog.

The Team Leader, Project Leader, or Project Manager often assume the Scrum Master role. Scrum provides this person with the structure to effectively carry out Scrum's new way of building systems. If it's likely that many impediments will have to be initially removed, this position may need to be filled by a senior manager or a Scrum consultant.

How does the Scrum Master keep the team working at the highest possible level of productivity? The Scrum Master does so primarily by making decisions and removing impediments. When decisions need to be made in the Daily Scrum, the Scrum Master is responsible for making the decisions immediately, even with incomplete information. I've found that it's usually better to proceed with some decision than no decision. The decision can always be reversed later, but in the meantime, the team can continue working. As for impediments, the Scrum Master either personally removes them or causes them to be removed as soon as possible. When the Scrum Master does the latter, he or she makes visible to the organization a policy, procedure, structure, or facility that is hurting productivity.

A Scrum Master has certain personality traits. He or she is usually focused and determined to do whatever is necessary for their Scrum teams. Some people aren't appropriate as Scrum Masters. They aren't comfortable being that visible and taking that much initiative. Removing impediments requires determination and stubbornness.

3.2   Product Backlog

> Product Backlog is an evolving, prioritized queue of business and technical functionality that needs to be developed into a system.
> —

The Scrum Master is responsible for employing the Scrum process to build a system or product. The requirements are listed in the Product Backlog. The Product Backlog represents everything that anyone interested in the product or process has thought is needed or would be a good idea in the product. It is a list of all features, functions, technologies, enhancements, and bug fixes that constitute the changes that will be made to the product for future releases. Anything that represents work to be done on the product is included in Product Backlog. These are examples of items that would go on the Product Backlog:

Allow users to access and view account balances for last six months.

Improve scalability of product.

Simplify installation process when multiple databases are used.

Determine how workflow can be added to product.

Product Backlog is initially incomplete, just an initial list of things that the product or system needs. The first Product Backlog may be a list of requirements that is gleaned from a vision document, garnered from a brainstorming session, or derived from a marketing requirements document. Sources of Product Backlog are as formal or informal as the hosting organization. To get the first Sprint going, Product Backlog only needs to contain enough requirements to drive a thirty-day Sprint. A Sprint can start from only concepts and a wish list.

The Product Backlog emerges from this initial list as the product and the customer's understanding of their needs emerge and evolve. Backlog is dynamic. Management repeatedly changes it to identify what the product requires to be appropriate, competitive, and useful. As long as a product exists, Product Backlog also exists.

Backlog originates from many sources. Product marketing generates features and functions. Sales generates backlog that will cause the product to be more competitive or please a particular customer. Engineering generates backlog that builds technology that holds the whole product together. Customer Support generates backlog to fix major product flaws.

Product Backlog is sorted in order of priority. Top priority Product Backlog drives immediate development activities. The higher a backlog item's priority, the more urgent it is, the more it has been thought about, and the more consensus there is regarding its value. Higher priority backlog is clearer and has more detailed specification than lower priority backlog. Better estimates are made based on the greater clarity and increased detail. The lower the priority, the less the detail, until you can barely make out the backlog item.

In addition to product features and technology, backlog items include issues. Issues require resolution before one or more backlog items can be worked on. For example, if response time is erratic and becoming a hot topic in the industry press, then this might be included as an issue in the Backlog. This issue is not ready to be defined as something to develop. However, it needs to be dealt with and perhaps turned into Product Backlog in the form of features or technology to be developed. Issues are prioritized, just like regular Product Backlog. The Product Owner is responsible for turning issues into work that the Scrum Team selects for a Sprint. Until he or she converts the issue to regular Product Backlog, it remains as "unworkable" Product Backlog. This ensures that the team isn't swamped by having to think about outstanding issues while it works.

As a product is used, as its value increases, and as the marketplace provides feedback, the product's backlog emerges into a larger and more comprehensive list. Requirements never stop changing. It makes little sense to pretend that this is not the case and attempt to set requirements in stone before beginning design and construction.

All you need is a product vision and enough top priority items on the backlog to begin one iteration, or Sprint, of incremental development on the product.

3.2.1   Product Owner Solely Controls the Product Backlog

Only one person is responsible for managing and controlling the Product Backlog. This person is referred to as the Product Owner. For commercial development, the Product Owner may be the product manager. For in-house development efforts, the Product Owner could be the project manager or the user department manager. This is the person who is officially responsible for the project. This person maintains the Product Backlog and ensures that it is visible to everyone. Everyone knows what items have the highest priority, so everyone knows what will be worked on.

The Product Owner is one person, not a committee. Committees may exist that advise or influence this person, but any person or body of people wanting an item's priority changed has to convince the Product Owner to make the change. Organizations have many ways of setting priorities and requirements. These practices will be influenced by Scrum across time, particularly through the meeting that reviews product increments (Sprint Review). The practice Scrum adds is that only one person is responsible for maintaining and sustaining the content and priority of a single Product Backlog. Otherwise, multiple conflicting lists flourish and the Scrum teams don't know which list to listen to. Without a single Product Owner, floundering, spin, contention, and frustration result.

For the Product Owner to succeed, everyone in the organization has to respect his or her decisions. No one is allowed to tell the Scrum Teams to work from a different set of priorities, and Scrum Teams aren't allowed to listen to anyone who says otherwise. All of the decisions that the Product Owner makes are highly visible, as they are reflected in the prioritization of the Product Backlog. This visibility requires the Product Owner to do his or her best, and makes the role of Product Owner both a demanding and a rewarding one.

3.2.2   Estimating Backlog Effort

As backlog is created, the Product Owner works with others to estimate how long it will take to develop. To reach the estimate, he or she talks to the developers, technical writers, quality control staff, and other people who understand the product and technology. This estimate includes the time it takes to perform all of the requisite architecture, design, construction and testing. The estimate will be as accurate as the Product Owner and team are at estimating; this means that the accuracy may vary wildly until the team becomes experienced at estimating. Since the team will build the backlog into code, their estimate is the best available.

Estimating is an iterative process. Estimates change as more information emerges about the backlog item and the item becomes better understood. Because higher priority backlog is better understood, the time estimates for these items are usually more accurate. If the Product Owner can't get a clear, believable estimate for a top priority backlog, he or she should consider redefining the backlog item, lowering its priority, or making it an issue instead of work.

The Product Backlog estimate is not binding on the Scrum team. The estimate does not mean, "this is how much time there is to build this functionality, and no more." The estimate is a starting point, a best guess, from which the Sprint can be empirically constructed and managed. The Scrum team selects the amount of Product Backlog that it believes it can handle in a Sprint based on these estimates. If the Product Owner hasn't worked with the team to create realistic estimates, the amount of Product Backlog selected may differ significantly from expectations.

Starting with the top priority backlog, the Product Owner develops estimates for each item. As the project gets underway, more will be known about available components, the utility of development tools, and the capability of the team. The estimates can then be revised.

3.3   Scrum Teams

> A team commits to achieving a Sprint goal. The team is accorded full authority to do whatever it decides is necessary to achieve the goal.   —

The Scrum Master meets with the Scrum Team and reviews the Product Backlog. The Scrum Team commits to turn a selected set of Product Backlog into a working product. The Scrum team makes this commitment every Sprint. The team has full authority to do whatever is necessary to do so. It is only constrained by organizational standards and conventions. Show it what to do, and it will figure out how to do it. Over time, teams get used to Scrum and begin committing to more and more work.

3.3.1   Team Dynamics

Every individual has their own strengths and weaknesses, comes from a unique background, and is trained and gains skills through a unique education and job history. Mix these individuals into a small team and you gain the strengths of team dynamics. You also can anticipate prejudice, resentments, petty squabbles, and all of the other negative attributes of human relationships. The team's commitment to produce a product increment each Sprint leads it to solve differences and draw on strengths.

A team member once came to see me to complain about a fellow team member who was encountering family problems. He was very upset and wanted the person removed from the team. I asked him if the team was better off with or without the person, if the person was contributing anything of value. He conceded that there were valuable contributions, but it was unfair that the other team member was distracted. I asked if he thought this other team member could do better, given the circumstances. He agreed that if he were in a similar situation, he would have a similar problem focusing. He also granted that he had worked with the fellow team member before and found him worthwhile. Our discussion led him to understand that this person was doing the level best he could, everything taken into consideration.

Scrum is structured to provide teams an environment within which they can do their best. Since the team commits to goals, the team members are often frustrated when things happen that undercut their commitments and anticipations. However, Scrum is empirical, and the team can reduce functionality and still meet goals, and management can adjust based on the product increment delivered at the end of the Sprint. In my experience, a team self-organizes to draw on its strengths rather than succumb to its problems. Each team member's best changes day by day, but the team's best tends to be rather predictable.

As a Scrum Master, I'm often tempted to help a team resolve its internal problems. Experience has taught me not to. The team has committed to a goal. When I help them resolve differences, I'm taking some of their responsibility away. The team committed to the goal; the team gets to figure out how to meet the goal, as best they can.

3.3.2   Team Size

The size of the team should be seven people, plus or minus two [Miller]. Teams as small as three can benefit, but the small size limits the amount of interaction that can occur and reduces productivity gains. Teams larger than eight don't work out well. Team productivity decreases and the Scrum's control mechanisms become cumbersome. Leading Daily Scrum meeting may become too difficult for the Scrum Master if the team is too large. Most importantly, large teams generate too much complexity for an empirical process.

If more than eight people are available, I strongly recommend breaking them into multiple teams. Identify one team. Let it select backlog and make a commitment for a Sprint. Then form another team. Let it select from the remaining backlog, commit, and proceed to Sprint. Based on each team's expertise, it will select the priority Product Backlog that it can best handle. Minimize the interaction and dependencies between the teams and maximize the cohesion of the work within each team. Make sure that the members of each team are working on things related to what their fellow team members are working on. I have managed product development with up to ten teams, coordinating their work with a daily "Scrum of Scrums." Scrum Masters from each team meet after the Daily Scrums for their own Daily Scrum.

3.3.3 Team Composition

Teams are cross functional. A Scrum Team should include people with all of the skills necessary to meet the Sprint goal. Scrum eschews vertical teams of analysts, designers, quality control, and coding engineers. A Scrum Team self-organizes so that everyone contributes to the outcome. Each team member applies his or her expertise to all of the problems. The resultant synergy from a tester helping a designer construct code improves code quality and raises productivity.

A team selects the amount of Product Backlog and establishes the Sprint goal. In most development processes, a manager tells each team member what to do and how long to take to do it. How can managers make this commitment for teams? In Scrum, no third party can commit a person or team to do work.

Who should be on a Scrum Team? I prefer to have at least one very experienced engineer as part of the team. They mentor junior engineers. During each Sprint, a team is required to test what it builds. Some teams include quality assurance testers to do testing. Other teams make the regular engineers test their own code. A technical writer is often included on a team. When no writer is assigned, engineers write rough user documentation themselves. Regardless of the team composition, it is responsible for doing all of the analysis, design, coding, testing, and user documentation.

Most team members are assigned full time to the team. Other team members are part time. Someone with particular domain or technical knowledge may not be available full time. Some team members aren't needed full time, such as a systems administrator or database administrator. When a team member commits to work on a Sprint, he or she commits based on what work can be done given the hours he or she is assigned to the team. Each team member knows his or her availability when making commitments. The team is interested in results and increments of product, not in time management. With time and experience, a team's skills in accurately estimating what it can do in a Sprint improves. The skill improves as the team learns the domain and the technology. The accuracy improves as the team realizes that Scrum does protect it from interference and interruptions.

There are no titles on teams. Teams self-organize to turn the requirements and technology into product functionality. This type of stateless, ego-less, development team is flexible to address any work that arises. Scrum avoids people who refuse to code because they are systems architects, or designers. Everyone chips in and does his or her best, doing or learning how to do what is needed. Scrum Team members don't have job descriptions other than doing the best possible. No titles, no exceptions.

Team composition may change at the end of a Sprint. The Scrum Master or Project Manager may choose to bring some new team members with more specific expertise or advanced capabilities. Management can also trade out under-performers and problem employees. Every time team membership is changed, the productivity gained from self-organization is diminished. I recommend that care be taken when changing team composition.

3.3.4   Team Responsibilities and Authority

The team is responsible for meeting the goal to which it commits at a Sprint planning meeting. The amount of backlog it will address is solely up to the team. Only the team can assess what it can accomplish over the next thirty days. The team has the authority to make any decisions, do whatever it needs to do, and ask for any impediments to be removed. Most organizations have no trouble holding people responsible. Management is sometimes surprised when a team assumes the authority necessary to meet their commitments. During a Scrum, only the team can define its work. The team may turn to others for advice and counseling, but it can take or reject whatever advice is offered. A team often goes through a short period during which it doesn't understand that it has full authority. It too is shocked and incredulous to find out that nobody else is going to tell it what to do. This surprise quickly disappears and the productivity of self-organization takes hold.

Although a team has the authority to decide how to do its work, the team is responsible for using and conforming to any existing charters, standards, conventions, architectures, and technology. These ensure that the products of the project and the Scrum Team fit in with other organizational products and can be understood by others. These charters, standards and conventions must be in place prior to the start of a Sprint.

If the team ever feels that it doesn't have the authority to meet the goals to which it committed, the team can call for an abnormal Sprint termination. The team calls for another Sprint Planning meeting. This is quite dramatic! The team found that assumptions it made during the Sprint planning meeting were incorrect and that it can't proceed.

3.3.5   Working Environment

It is important to equip a team with the best possible tools. It's incredibly shortsighted to take expensive engineers performing important work and to hobble them with inadequate tools and infrastructure. One team I worked with needed workstations for the contractors. I requisitioned them. The workstations arrived with 15-inch monitors, the organizational standard. The team was doing multiple-window development and 15-inch monitors would require constant task switching to keep the most current work on top. A larger monitor would be better. The distributor returned within two hours with the larger monitors. I then worked with management to change the workstation standard.

Use open working environments. Such environments allow people to communicate more easily, make it easier to get together, and facilitate self-organization. When I walk into open team areas, I can immediately tell how the team is doing. Silence is always a bad sign. I know that people are collaborating if I can hear conversations. When I enter a cubicle environment, there is often silence, indicating an absence of interaction. Cubicles are truly the bane of the modern workplace. They quite literally keep people apart and break teams up.

If I were starting another software company, I'd gut whatever space I had, put in wood or concrete floors, cover the walls with whiteboards, and scatter telephone and network connections throughout. Then I'd issue everyone a rolling desk, a rolling file cabinet, and a cart with a computer and monitor. I'd let people form their own work groups, clusters of furniture formed on the basis of who was working with whom at the time. I've been in facilities like these, and they're fantastic. You can hear the hum of activity and feel the energy in the air. It is always obvious that good things are happening at these places. Of course, not every company is able, or even willing, to make this kind of renovation. There are other ways to facilitate teamwork by changing layout, though. At a company without enough conference rooms, I turned several offices into one team room. Once the team moved into its new room, productivity skyrocketed.

A Scrum Team sets its own working hours, though it is subject to some constraints. Teams are responsible for not disrupting the organizational environment (such as working from 10pm to 6am daily). However, the organization owes it to the team to let it figure out when it can work best. Also, team members need to work when the rest of the team is present.

3.4 Daily Scrum Meetings

> Software development is a complex process that requires lots of communications. The Daily Scrum meeting is where the team comes to communicate.   —

Each Scrum Team meets daily for a 15-minute status meeting called the Daily Scrum. During the meeting, the team explains what it has accomplished since the last meeting, what it is going to do before the next meeting, and what obstacles are in its way. The Daily Scrum meeting gets people used to team-based, rapid, intense, co-operative, courteous development. Daily Scrums improve communications, eliminate other meetings, identify and remove impediments to development, highlight and promote quick decision-making, and improve everyone's level of project knowledge. That's a lot of benefit from just 15 minutes a day! An impediment I hear over and over is that team members have to attend status meetings. I tell the team not to go to these other status meetings. Anyone who needs to know what's going on with the project can come to the Daily Scrum and listen.

The Scrum Master is responsible for successfully conducting the Daily Scrum. The Scrum Master keeps the Daily Scrum short by enforcing the rules and making sure that people speak briefly. This requires a fair amount of courage since the rules apply equally to everyone. It's difficult to tell a Senior Vice President not to interrupt.

By listening carefully during a Daily Scrum meeting, managers can get a sense of what the team is doing and how likely it is to succeed. Attending a Daily Scrum is easier and more informative than reading a report, and Daily Scrums have the additional benefit of being a boon for the team as well as for its managers. Scrum is direct and open. Because the reporting interval is only 24 hours, it's easy to continuously monitor a team. A Scrum Master can quickly see if a team member is up to his or her ears trying to get a piece of technology to work. Has a team member lost interest in the project? Is someone not working because of family problems? Is the team quarreling over something? What attitudes are demonstrated during the meeting?

> I was once given a very tasteful conference room to use as a Scrum Room. I knew it was tasteful because it had paintings on the walls but no whiteboards. I requested whiteboards for a whole month, but my requests were ignored. Finally, I improvised: I started using sticky flip chart paper. This is a fantastic product: you write on a flip chart pad, tear off the pages you want to keep, and stick them to the wall with adhesive on the back of each page. One day I ran out of paper on the pad. I looked around, but couldn't find anything else to use. Finally, I took down a picture and started writing on the walls with magic marker. Pretty soon the walls were covered with writing. Everyone came to see, aghast that this social taboo had been violated. The Facilities Department heard about this, of course, and responded by repainting the walls and (finally!) installing whiteboards. The moral of this story is that you should use your facilities as best you can to keep your productivity high.

3.4.1 Establishing a Meeting Room

The Scrum Master should establish a meeting place and time for the Daily Scrum. The room in which the Daily Scrum is held is called the Scrum Room. The team holds its Daily Scrum in this room every working day at the same place and same time. The room should be readily accessible from the team's primary working location. It should be equipped with a door (to close during the meeting), a speakerphone (for team members who will attend by calling-in), a table, at least enough chairs for each team member to sit around the table, and white boards (for recording notes, issues, and impediments and for general brainstorming after the Daily Scrum). Of course, Scrum has been successfully implemented in environments that did not have well appointed Scrum Rooms. The most important thing is that the time and location of the Daily Scrum be constant. I've started out by holding Daily Scrums in the corner of a cafeteria, on a lawn, and even in a neighboring coffee shop. It is only a matter of time before management sees the value of the Daily Scrum and rushes to provide a Scrum Room, or if management has already provided one, to improve the facilities in the Scrum Room.

> A chicken and a pig are together when the
> chicken says, "Let's start a restaurant!"
> The pig thinks it over and says, "What
> would we call this restaurant?" The chicken
> says, "Ham n' Eggs!"
> The pig says, "No, thanks. I'd be commit-
> ted, but you'd only be involved!"

3.4.2   Chickens and Pigs

Team members commit to a goal and do the work that is required to meet it.
They are called pigs because they, like the pigs in the joke, are committed
to the project. Everyone else is a chicken. Chickens can attend Daily
Scrums, but they have to stand on the periphery. Chickens are not allowed
to interfere with the meeting in any way, such as talking, gesticulating, or
making noise. Chickens are present as guests and must follow Scrum rules.

I once implemented Scrum at an organization that published trade
journals on the Web, starting with just one team for one magazine. Everyone else wanted to find out how Scrum worked, though, so I invited them
to the Daily Scrum. Soon over thirty chickens were in the room. Any room
with that many people has too much movement and too many distractions.
There are many chickens that need to be present at the Daily Scrums, including those who need to keep track of the Sprint - such as users, product
managers, and management. But the Daily Scrum is not a spectacle. Keep
attendance to a minimum. I suggest you not use a team's Daily Scrum as
a sort of training program for others teams.

3.4.3   Starting the Meeting

The Scrum Master is responsible for ensuring that the Daily Scrum goes
well. Scrum Masters ensure that the room is setup for the meeting. They
get any team members working from remote locations set up on a conference phone before the meeting starts[1]. Also, they work to minimize the
distractions that occur during the meeting so everyone can stay focused
and the meeting can be kept short. For example, a good Scrum Master
might even set the chairs up around the table before the meeting begins so
that people don't get caught up in side conversations as they move chairs
around. The Scrum Master's job is to increase the productivity of the
team in any way possible. Arranging chairs is one small demonstration of
commitment.

---

[1] "Paul Martin had a daily Scrum in his office which was so small everyone had to
stand up. A third of the team was in his office, a third in Burlington, and a third in
Seattle. This was one of the best running Scrums I have seen. It produced the web
framework for all of IDX's products." Jeff Sutherland, 2001. (Private Correspondance.)

The team should arrange themselves in a circle, generally around a focus such as a table. Some Scrum Teams sit, while others have found that standing encourages brevity. Team members seat themselves in any order as they arrive. People not on the team sit or stand around the periphery, outside of the team circle. When guests sit around the table, or interject themselves into the team circle, they feel free to interject comments and to have side conversations. This makes it hard to control the meeting duration. If chickens are placed outside the circle, they are physically reminded that they are observers, and not participants.

Every team member must arrive on time for each Daily Scrum. The meeting starts promptly at the designated time, regardless of who is or is not present. Many Scrum Masters highlight the importance of promptness by imposing a small fine for tardiness. Any team member who doesn't attend or doesn't show up on time is fined $1, which is collected immediately by the Scrum Master. This money is periodically given to a charity.

3.4.4   Format of the Daily Scrum

During the Daily Scrum, only one person – from the pigs – talks at a time. That person is the one who is reporting his or her status. Everyone else listens. There are no side conversations. Starting to his or her immediate left, the Scrum Master goes around the room and asks team members to answer three questions.

What have you done since last Scrum? This question addresses only the last 24 hours, unless a weekend or holiday has occurred in the interim. Team members only mention the things they have done that relate to this team and this Sprint. For example, the team isn't interested in other work that part-timers might be doing unless it relates directly to their own work. If team members are doing work other than what they had planned to be doing for this Sprint, that other work should be identified as an impediment. Anything not related to the team's work is probably an impediment.

What will you do between now and the next Scrum? This question relates only to this Sprint and this team. What is each team member planning to work on? The work a team member expects to do should match the work that has been planned by the team. If team members state they are going to be doing other work, they should be asked why. The team might need to meet after the Daily Scrum to talk about the new work. Other team members have to adjust their work based on the new work. Getting answers to these questions can help the team and management assess whether the work is proceeding regularly and as expected, or if adjustments are needed.

What got in your way of doing work? If a team member was unable to work or anticipates being unable to work on what he or she planned, what got in his or her way? That is to say, what is getting in the way of the team? Each team member has planned and committed to a goal and is empirically figuring out the work to meet the goal. What is slowing down individual team members, and therefore the team as a whole? Although team members have worked within the organization and are used to its culture and style, the Scrum Master should encourage them to think "outside of the box." If this were the perfect work environment, what else would it have? More specifically, what could help the team be more productive, both as a group of individuals and as a cohesive team?

Team members should keep their responses to these questions brief and to the point. They shouldn't elaborate or describe how the work was done or will be done unless they want to highlight help they may need. For instance, a team member may report that he or she intends to complete implementing a feature in a module, but he or she is having difficulty understanding how a specific algorithm works. Or the team member may report that he or she is going to check in some code but can't get the source code management system to work without crashing.

The Daily Scrum is not a design session and should not turn into a working session. Don't discuss design or start to solve a problem. There isn't enough time or flexibility in the Daily Scrum to begin working through issues of this magnitude. By limiting the meeting's scope, the Scrum Master can keep the duration in check and constant. If the scope of the Daily Scrum expands, no one will know how much time to allocate to the meeting.

3.4.5   Identifying Impediments

If a team member identifies something that is stopping him or her from working effectively, the Scrum Master is responsible for recording and removing that impediment. Impediments should be written down on the white board on the wall. If the Scrum Master doesn't fully understand the impediment, he or she should meet with whoever mentioned it after the Scrum Meeting to learn about it. The following are common impediments:

Workstation, network, and/or server are down

Network or server are slow

Required to attend human resource training session

Required to attend status meeting with management

Asked by management to do something else

Asked to do something other than what this team member committed to for this Sprint.

Unsure about how to proceed

Unsure of design decision

Unsure how to use technology

The Scrum Master's top priority is removing impediments. If team members inform the Scrum Master that he or she can do something to make them more productive, the Scrum Master should do it. The Daily Scrum gives the Scrum Master direct information on what he or she can do to improve the productivity of the team.

If the impediments aren't promptly resolved, the team will report the next day that it is still impeded. It is a bad sign if the team members stop reporting impediments even though they haven't been resolved. This usually means that the team members have lost their confidence that the Scrum Master can and will resolve their impediments. If, for some good reason, an impediment cannot be removed, the Scrum Master should report on this at the next Daily Scrum.

If the open impediments on the white board get to be lengthy, this may indicate that the larger organization isn't supporting the team. In this case, the Scrum Master may have to cancel the Sprint. This is a very powerful card to play. It should be played only when the Scrum Master is very concerned that the organization's support for the project is so low as to render the team ineffective. Low support could be because this is an unimportant project or because the organization is unable to effectively support any projects. The reason doesn't matter to this project. The Scrum Master has observed that there are many impediments and management is unwilling or unable to remove them. The Scrum Master should very carefully and intensely discuss these observations and the consequences of the lack of support with management before canceling the Sprint. Once the decision has been made to cancel the Sprint, the Scrum Master is effectively stating that there isn't enough management support or organizational effectiveness for the project to succeed. See the later section on *"Abnormal Termination of Sprints"* for more details.

3.4.6   Making Decisions

A Scrum team has full authority to make all of the decisions necessary to turn the Product Backlog into a Product Increment to meet the Sprint Goal. The team is free to do whatever is necessary to make the best decision possible and do the best work. The team members can interview others, bring in consultants, read books, browse the web, or whatever they need (within budgetary constraints). A team member may identify indecision as an impediment (e.g. "I don't know if I should do this or that."). The Scrum Master is then responsible for making a decision, preferably then and there. When first implementing Scrum for a team, the Scrum Master should be careful not to make too many decisions for the team. Delegated decision-making is new in most organizations. The Scrum Master helps the team learn to make its own decisions to fulfill its commitments. The more the team relies on outsiders to make its decisions, the less control it has over its commitments.

When the team is uncertain, it should acquire whatever information is necessary to become more certain. Sometimes a team asks for someone else to make a decision because it feels that the decision is risky, or sensitive. In this case, the Scrum Master should meet with the team after the Daily Scrum and work through to a decision. A team should make a decision by acting on the best information that it has and by relying on its instincts. Most snap decisions are more acceptable than holding up work to wait for someone else to decide. The team usually has a far better handle on the alternatives than anyone else. Also, completed work has momentum and usually will be "good enough," or at the very least, it will be far better than nothing.

Most of the time the decision will be acceptable. Sometimes, though, a decision results in unacceptable product functionality or application of technology. This becomes apparent when the product increment is reviewed at the end of the Sprint. If an incorrect decision isn't visible at this review, it is probably irrelevant. Otherwise work can be redone to correct the bad decision. Because Sprints are so short, bad decisions rarely impact more than thirty days worth of work.

If the Scrum Master can't make a decision during the meeting, he or she is responsible for making a decision and communicating it to the whole team within one hour after the end of the Scrum.

3.4.7   Establishing Follow-Up Meetings

If any discussion is needed other than the status provided by answering the three questions, a follow-up meeting may be requested. After a team member gives his or her status, another team member can interject, "I'd like to address this more after the Scrum. Anyone who's interested should hang around afterward." More than one team member may want to address the topic in more depth. This conversation may get into discussing design or requirements alternatives or interpretations. A team member may be working on the same thing and wants to share information. This sharing will be of indeterminate length and may lead to design discussions. A team member may have done something like this before or may know an easier way to do the work. This may lead to another team member suggesting another approach, resulting in a design discussion. A working meeting is needed to reach a decision or to discuss design or standards. In each of these cases, the conversation that starts is open-ended. Other team members may join in and more time will go by. All of these discussions are worthwhile and should happen. They should happen after the Daily Scrum, though. Keep all working sessions outside of the Daily Scrum, or else the distinction between a status session and a working session will become blurred and the time for the Scrum won't remain short and fixed.

3.5   Sprint Planning Meeting

Customers, users, management, the Product Owner and the Scrum Team determine the next Sprint goal and functionality at the Sprint Planning meeting. The team then devises the individual tasks that must be performed to build the product increment.
—

3.5.1   Sprint Planning Meeting Overview

Scrum Teams meet with the Scrum Master and others to plan each Sprint. The Sprint planning meeting actually consists of two consecutive meetings. At the first meeting, the team meets with the Product Owner, management, and users to figure out what functionality to build during the next Sprint. At the second meeting, the team works by itself to figure out how it is going to build this functionality into a product increment during the Sprint. Input to this meeting is the Product Backlog, the latest increment of product, and the capabilities and past performance of the team. See figure 3.1 for an overview of planning a new Sprint.

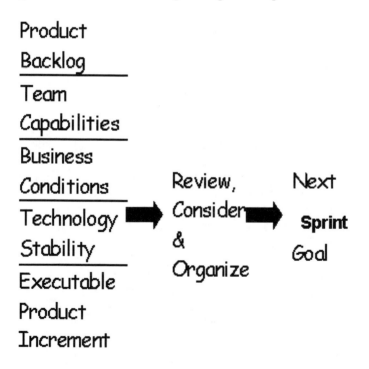

FIGURE 3.1: Input for new Sprint

3.5.2   Identify Product Backlog and Goal for Next Sprint

To start the meeting, the Product Owner presents the top priority Product Backlog. He or she leads a discussion about what changes to the backlog are appropriate, given what was demonstrated at the end of the previous Sprint (see *Sprint Review*). What does everyone want the team to work on next? Working with the Product Owner, management, and customers, the team identifies the Product Backlog that it believes it can develop during the next Sprint (30 calendar days).

These are examples of top priority Product Backlog:

Implement a middleware alternative for providing secure, recoverable access by applications to legacy databases

The client account modification functionality in the account management system loses transactions when it or the databases crash. Secure these transactions.

The client account modification functionality has to identify "high value" accounts in real-time

The Product Backlog is a mix of functionality and technology. The first backlog item could have been more precise if the technology already had been decided upon. For example, it could have read:

"Implement an object-oriented middleware connection between applications and legacy databases that is secure and recoverable using Tuxedo from BEA systems and using CORBA-compliant wrappers."

In the absence of directions to the contrary, the team is free to choose how it implements the functionality. In this example, the team only selected the first, highest priority, Product Backlog. The team has committed to attempt to implement this functionality on some new technology. The team, of course, doesn't know exactly what can be done, how amenable the technology will be, or how difficult or simple the functionality will be.

Having selected the Product Backlog, a Sprint Goal is crafted. The Sprint Goal is an objective that will be met through the implementation of the Product Backlog. For instance, this Sprint Goal could be:

Sprint Goal: to provide a standardized middleware mechanism for the identified customer service transactions to access backend databases.

The reason for having a Sprint Goal is to give the team some wiggle room regarding the functionality. For example, the goal for the above Sprint could also be: "Automate the client account modification functionality through a secure, recoverable transaction middleware capability." As the team works, it keeps this goal in mind. In order to satisfy the goal, it implements the functionality and technology. If the work turns out to be harder than the team had expected, then the team might only partially implement the functionality. At the Sprint Review meeting, management, customers, and the Product Owner review how and to what degree the functionality has been implemented. They review how the Sprint Goal has been met. If they are dissatisfied, they can then make decisions about requirements, technology or team composition. During the Sprint, though, the team alone determines how to meet the Sprint Goal. At the end of the Sprint, any incomplete work returns to the Product Backlog.

3.5.3   Define Sprint Backlog to Meet Sprint Goal

After establishing the Sprint goal, the team determines what work will have to be performed in order to reach the goal. All team members are required to be present when this is determined. The team may also invite other people to attend in order to provide technical or domain advice. The Product Owner often attends. A new team often first realizes that it will either sink or swim as a team, not individually, in this meeting. The team realizes that it must rely on its own ingenuity, creativity, cooperation, collaboration, and effort. As it realizes this, it starts to self-organize to take on the characteristics and behavior of a real team. During this meeting, management and the user should not do or say anything that takes the team off the hook or makes its decisions for it.

The team compiles a list of tasks it has to complete to meet the Sprint goal. These tasks are the detailed pieces of work needed to convert the Product Backlog into working software. Tasks should have enough detail so that each task takes roughly four to sixteen hours to finish. This task list is called the Sprint Backlog. The team self-organizes to assign and undertake the work in the Sprint Backlog. Sometimes only a partial Sprint Backlog can be created. The team may have to define an initial architecture or create designs before it can fully delineate the rest of the tasks. In such a case, the team should define the initial investigation, design, and architecture work in as much detail as possible, and leave reminders for work that will probably have to be done once the investigation or design has been completed. At that time, the work will be more fully understood and another team meeting can be convened to detail it.

To meet the above Sprint Goal, some of the Sprint Backlog that the team might devise is:

Map the transaction elements to back-end database tables.

Write a business object in C++ to handle transactions via defined methods and interfaces.

Wrap the C++ in a CORBA wrapper.

Use Tuxedo for all queuing, messaging, and transaction management.

Measure the transaction performance to determine whether scalability requirements can be met.

The team modifies Sprint Backlog throughout the Sprint. As it gets into individual tasks, it may find out that more or fewer tasks are needed, or that a given task will take more or less time than had been expected. As new work is required, the team adds it to the Sprint Backlog. As tasks are worked on or completed, the hours of estimated remaining work for each task is updated. When tasks are deemed unnecessary, they are removed. Only the team can change its Sprint Backlog during a Sprint. Only the team can change the contents or the estimates. The Sprint Backlog is a highly visible, real time picture of the work that the team plans to accomplish during the Sprint, and it belongs solely to the team.

Sometimes the Scrum Team discovers that it has selected too much Product Backlog to complete in a single Sprint. If this happens, the Scrum Master immediately meets with the Product Owner and the Scrum team. They collectively identify Product Backlog that can be removed while still meeting the Sprint Goal. If no backlog can be removed, they work together to identify functionality with scope or depth that can be lessened.

Teams become better at Sprint planning after the third or fourth Sprint. At first, a team tends to be nervous about taking on responsibility and it under-commits. As it becomes more familiar with Scrum processes, as it starts to understand the functionality and technology, and as it gels into a team, it commits to more work.

3.6   Sprint

The team works for a fixed period of time called a Sprint.   —

The Scrum Team has decided what it will accomplish during the upcoming Sprint. It now sprints to accomplish the Sprint Goal. The team is free to accomplish this goal as it sees fit, adapting to the circumstances, technology, and organizational terrain as best it can.

During conflicts, the military will put teams of soldiers into insertion points in areas of operations. Each team is assigned a mission to accomplish and self-organizes to accomplish it. The team has all the supplies and training that it is expected to need. Since the insertion point is usually in the middle of a complex, even chaotic, situation, the team's knowledge of the situation or what to do to reach the goal is limited to a game plan. The team is intended to improvise in order to accomplish its mission. At some predetermined time, the mission ends and the team is picked up.

Scrum was first described in similar terms [Takeuchi and Nonaka]: "Typically, the process starts with management giving the project team a broad goal. Rarely do they hand out a clear-cut new product concept or a specific work plan. Thus, while the project team has extreme freedom, it is also faced with extreme challenges embodied within the goal. The project team is typically driven to a state of 'zero information' as the extent of the challenge essentially makes prior knowledge inapplicable. Thus the team must fend for itself and find a way to coalesce into a dynamic group."

"According to several of the companies surveyed, the process tends to produce significant quantities of mistakes. However, these are viewed invariably from the plus side as being valuable learning experiences. In the end, the bottom line is that the chaotic process tends to produce more revolutionary products faster than the old sequential development process. It also tends to develop the project team members into 'triple threat' players as each person's knowledge base is broadly expanded through their interaction."

3.6.1   Product Increments Are Mined from Chaos

After the overall goals and objectives are established at the Sprint planning meeting, the Scrum Team is dropped into the insertion point for a Sprint. The team is asked to do its best to turn the complex requirements and unpredictable technology into a product increment. It is asked to tame chaos, to turn complexity into predictable product. What a job!

Scrum asks people to try to wrest a predictable product from unpredictable complexity. Some people can't handle this type of assignment. During the Sprint, they may decide that they want out. Other people relish the chance to build something that requires their best effort. Those who succeed at Scrum are the individuals that will form the core of an organization. Scrum helps identify these people.

Management has invested thirty days of a team in the Sprint. Regardless of what the team accomplishes, it has acquired valuable working knowledge of the requirements and technology. Even when the team produces nothing tangible, it has nonetheless gone through a very useful learning process. The team has trained itself to take another crack at a reconstituted Sprint goal. It has a deeper understanding of the terrain and complexity, and is better equipped for success.

3.6.2   No Interference, No Intruders, No Peddlers

A team is let loose for the thirty day Sprint. The team has committed to the goal and accepted the responsibility of building a product increment that meets the goal. It has the authority to act as it sees fit. No person outside the team can change the scope or nature of the work the team is doing during a Sprint. No one is allowed to add more functionality or technology to the Sprint. No one can tell the team how to proceed in its work. This really is like the military insertion point.

Many organizations are initially uncomfortable with the idea of letting a team loose for a Sprint. It just doesn't feel right. It feels too risky. But, is it really so strange for management to trust a team of its own employees to figure out the best and most appropriate things to do? How much of a risk is this really? Management has assigned the best people available to the team. What the team will do is defined in the Sprint Goals and Product Backlog. The risk is limited to thirty calendar days of the team's Sprint. Management can see how the team's doing by attending Daily Scrums and, failing that, can always inspect the most recently updated version of the Sprint Backlog. At the end of the thirty days, management meets with the team. At the very worst, the team has built nothing but has learned much. More often, the team has built something that reflects its best efforts. The team often exceeds expectations. Once the creative juices get flowing, teams become hotbeds of creativity and productivity. A Sprint is management's bet that employees are capable and know what they are doing.

3.6.3 Sprint Mechanics

Sprints last for thirty calendar days. A team takes this long to get its arms around a problem and to produce a product increment. Management usually can't refrain from interfering if more than thirty days goes by, so the Sprint is limited to thirty days. First-time Scrum users usually want to change the length of the Sprint to, say, sixty days, two weeks, or one week. It is worth resisting this temptation. Thirty days is an excellent compromise between many competing pressures. Adjustments can be made to the duration after everyone has more experience with Scrum.

The team has complete authority during the Sprint. It can work as many hours or as few hours as it wants. It can hold meetings whenever it wants. It can hold design sessions from 6am to 10pm. It can spend days interviewing vendors and consultants, or surfing the web for information. The team has absolute authority, because management has given the team free reign for thirty days.

Every product development project is constrained by four variables, (1) time available, (2) cost, in people and resources, (3) delivered quality, and (4) delivered functionality. A Sprint greatly fixes the first three variables. The Sprint will always be thirty days long. The cost is pretty well fixed to the salaries of the team members and the development environment. This is usually in place before a Sprint starts. However, teams can add the cost of consultants or tools during Sprints to remove impediments if the budget is adhered to. Quality is usually an organizational standard. If it isn't, the team needs to devise quality targets prior to Sprinting.

The team has the authority to change the functionality of the Sprint so long as it meets its Sprint Goal. The team does this is by decreasing or increasing the scope or depth of the functionality delivered. For example, the team can change the depth of functionality to "check account balance." The team can implement this functionality by checking all possible accounts, or only one account. The design and code to perform each implementation is significantly different. At the Sprint Review meeting, the depth to which the functionality is implemented is demonstrated and discussed. Any remaining, unimplemented functionality is re-entered onto the Product Backlog and reprioritized.

The team has two mandatory accountabilities during the Sprint: (1) Daily Scrum meetings and (2) the Sprint Backlog. These are working tools for the team. Daily Scrum meetings must be promptly attended by all team members, whether in person or via telephone. Team members cannot just send in a passive status report, such as by email or fax. The Sprint Backlog must be kept up-to-date and as accurate as the team's activities, so that it constitutes an accurate and evolving picture of the team and the work that it is doing. As team members work on Sprint backlog, they adjust the estimates.

During the Sprint, all work that is performed is measured and empirically controlled. More or less work may end up being accomplished depending on how things proceed. Factors influencing the amount of work accomplished include the team's ability to work together, the skills of team members, the details of the work to be performed, and the capability of the tools and standards with which the team has been provided. Because Scrum allows the team to change the amount of work it performs during the Sprint, the team has some flexibility, and is able to do more or less so long as it meets its Sprint Goals.

The team is required to deliver a product increment at the end of the Sprint. Daily product builds are an excellent way for the team to measure its progress. Prior to the build, the team should update the test suite and follow each product build with a smoke, or regression, test. Performing code check-ins for the builds is also a good idea, as it improves team communication and coordination.

3.6.4   Abnormal termination of Sprints

Sprints can be cancelled before the allotted thirty days are over. Under what kind of circumstances might a Sprint need to be cancelled? Management may need to cancel a Sprint if the Sprint Goal becomes obsolete. A company as a whole may change direction. Market conditions or technological requirements might change. Management can simply change its mind. In general, a Sprint should be cancelled if it no longer makes sense given the circumstances. However, because of the short duration of Sprints, it rarely makes sense for management to cancel a Sprint.

Sometimes the team itself may decide that a Sprint should be cancelled. A team comes to better understand its abilities and the project's requirements during a Sprint. The team may realize mid-way through the Sprint that it cannot achieve its Sprint Goal. Even if the team's knowledge of its work has not changed, the Sprint could still need to be cancelled. For example, the team might run into a major roadblock. Sometimes, the team feels that it has met its Sprint goal, and decides to cancel the Sprint because it wants more direction from management before proceeding to implement more functionality.

That the team has the power to cancel its own Sprint is very important. The team is able to stay focused because it can terminate the Sprint if someone tries to change the nature or scope of its work. Everyone knows this, and is consequently reluctant to make any such changes. Sprint terminations consume resources, since everyone has to regroup in another Sprint planning meeting to start another Sprint. Usually, the first question that is asked when a Sprint is terminated is: "Who is responsible for this meeting occurring early?" Because people don't want to be named as the answer to this question, very few Sprints end up being terminated.

3.7   Sprint Review

> The Sprint Review meeting is a four-hour informational meeting. During this meeting, the team presents to management, customers, users, and the Product Owner the product increment that it has built during the Sprint.   —

Before the days of satellites and global positioning systems, ocean-going ships attempted to "fix" their position every morning and evening. The navigation officer measured the angle of three or more stars relative to the horizon, plotted the ship's position relative to each star, and found the intersection of the lines plotting the ship's relative positions to these stars. This was called the "fix." It determined a ship's true position, and "fixed" errors in previous estimations of the ship's location. Currents, wind, faulty steering mechanisms, and poor previous fixes might result in miles of difference between the ship's estimated and real position. During bad weather, fixes often couldn't be made for days at a time because of poor visibility, and the estimated position of the ship became progressively more wrong. As ships approached shore, they would often stay away from the coastline until a good fix could be obtained. The last fix was the best information possible, though, and the ship's officer would set the course based on it.

The Sprint Review provides a similar fix on a project. The team has estimated where it will be at the end of the Sprint and set its course accordingly. At the end of the Sprint, the team presents the product increment that it has been able to build. Management, customers, users, and the Product Owner assess the product increment. They listen to the tales the team has to tell about its journey during the Sprint. They hear what went wrong and what went right. They take a fix on where they really are on their voyage of building the product and system. After all of this, they are able to make an informed decision about what to do next. In other words, they determine the best course to take in order to reach their intended destination. Just like "shooting the stars" provides regularity to shipboard life, the thirty-day Sprint cycle provides a meaningful rhythm in the team's life and even in the company's life. The Sprint Review meeting happens every thirtieth day, and the team builds product during the other twenty-nine days.

Management comes to the Sprint Review to see what the team has been able to build with the resources that it has been given. Customers come to the Sprint Review to see if they like what the team has built. The Product Owner comes to the Sprint Review to see how much functionality has been built. Other engineers and developers come to the meeting to see what the team was able to do with the technology. Everyone wants to see what the team has built, what the Sprint was like, how the technology worked, what shortcuts had to be taken, what things it was able to add, and its ideas as to what can be done next.

The Scrum Master is responsible for coordinating and conducting the Sprint Review meeting. The Scrum Master meets with the team to establish the agenda and discuss how the Sprint results will be presented and by whom. The Scrum Master sends all attendants a reminder a week before the meeting, confirming the time, date, location, attendees, and agenda.

To prepare for the meeting, the team considers what attendees need to see in order to understand what has been developed during the Sprint. The team wants everyone to understand as many dimensions of the product increment as possible. What should attendants learn from this meeting? They should gain an understanding of the system and technical architecture and design that hold the product together, as well as the functionality that has been built onto the architecture. They should be familiarized with the strength and weaknesses of the design and technology so they will know what limitations to be taken into account, and what advantages to leverage when planning the next Sprint.

The best presentations usually start with the Scrum Master giving a concise overview of the Sprint. The Sprint goal and Product Backlog are compared to the actual results of the Sprint, and reasons for any discrepancies are discussed. A team member can display and review a simple product architecture diagram. The most effective architecture diagrams display both the technical and functional architecture. Previously completed technology and functions are highlighted on the diagram. Technology and functionality produced during the past Sprint are then added onto the diagram, and team members demonstrate the functionality as it is added to the diagram. For the most part, the Sprint Review meeting is held in just one place, but during the demonstration of product functionality, the meeting will often move from one workstation and office to another.

During the meeting, everyone visualizes the demonstrated product functionality working in the customer or user environment. As this is visualized, consider what functionality might be added in the next Sprint. The product increment is the focal point for brainstorming. For example, someone could suggest the following after seeing the product increment demonstrated: "If we did "controlled patient costs" manually, we could use this right now in registration!" or "This would solve the problems that we're having tracking inventory in the districts. What would we have to do to make this work off the inventory database?" As the team demonstrates the product increment, it helps the attendees understand the weaknesses and strengths of the product increments, and the difficulties and successes it experienced pulling it together.

No one should prepare extensively for the meeting. In order to enforce this rule, PowerPoint presentations and their ilk are forbidden. If the team feels that it has to spend more than two hours preparing for the meeting, then it usually has less to show for the Sprint than it had hoped, and it is trying to obscure this fact with a fancy presentation. Sprint Review Meetings are very informal. What matters is the product the team has been able to create. The Sprint Review is a working meeting. Questions, observations, discussions and suggestions are allowed and encouraged. If a lot of give and take is needed, it should happen. Remember, though, that the meeting is informational, not critical or action-oriented. Everyone should get an understanding of the product increment, as this is the knowledge they will need for the Sprint Planning meeting.

We have discussed the practices of Scrum. You should now have a good sense of what you need to do to run a Sprint with a Scrum team from the Product Backlog. In the next chapter, I'll discuss how to implement Scrum in your organization and manage a Scrum project.

CHAPTER 4

Applying Scrum

This section presents how to implement and manage Scrum within an organization. —

4.1 Implementing Scrum

If engineering practices are candy bars, then Scrum is a candy bar wrapper. That is to say that Scrum is superimposed on and encapsulates whatever engineering practices already exist. The ease of implementing Scrum often comes as a surprise. Implementing new practices, cultures, and methodologies is usually difficult, and can even be painful, but implementing Scrum is not. Scrum simplifies existing work by allowing a team and management to focus on just the next thirty days. Management practices such as pert charts, time reporting, and lengthy status meetings to control a project can be discarded.

Scrum changes how people think of work. As an organization uses Scrum, the roles that managers and workers within that organization play evolve. Managers begin to expedite more and do less paperwork. Workers become empowered and begin to focus more on their work. Scrum challenges practices and structures that get in the way of focused work. How organizations respond to the challenge of Scrum varies widely from organization to organization. But while an organization formulates its response, Scrum is letting it get the product out the door.

Managers are sometimes caught flat-footed by the changes that Scrum effects. When the Sprint starts, they feel like they have nothing to do: the team has taken over responsibility for figuring out what to do and is organizing itself to accomplish its goals. Then the manager's day starts filling up as the manager begins working the organization to remove impediments to the team's progress. The manager makes decisions during the daily Scrum, and then validates these decisions within the larger organization. The manager blocks interference and helps the team focus. The manager becomes a coach and a good friend to the team.

4.1.1 Implementing Scrum for New Projects

When I implement Scrum, I'm sometimes asked to start with a new project. I work with the team and customer for several days to devise a "starter" Product Backlog. The starter backlog consists of some business functionality and the technology requirements. To implement this functionality, the team designs and builds an initial system framework with the selected technology. The team implements user functionality into this framework. The team may have to connect the functionality to a preliminary or existing database. Under these circumstances, the goal for the first Sprint is:

"Demonstrate a key piece of user functionality on the selected technology."

When the team defines the Sprint Backlog to meet this goal, it includes tasks necessary to build the development environment, set up the team, employ code management and build management practices, implement the target system technology on a test platform, and build the functionality. This constitutes a pretty full Sprint.

This initial Sprint has two purposes. First, the team needs to settle into a development environment in which it can construct functionality. Second, the team builds a working part of the system to demonstrate to the customer within thirty days. Demonstrating functionality this quickly invigorates customer involvement and thinking. The customer realizes the system is for real, right now, and thinks, "Now that the system is really being built, I'd better decide what I want from it. I'd better get involved!" The first Sprint gets the team and customer into a regular thirty-day rhythm of defining and delivering, defining and delivering.

While the team is working on the first Sprint, the Product Owner and customers build more Product Backlog. The Product Backlog doesn't have to be complete; it only needs to include enough top priority items to drive the next few Sprints. As the Product Owner and customers get a feel for Scrum, they start taking a longer view of Product Backlog. If a system or product vision isn't available, the Product Owner and customer will forge one. They will then construct Product Backlog on the basis of this vision.

4.1.2   Implementing Scrum for Ongoing Projects

I'm often called upon to use Scrum to get an existing project or product development effort focused, productive, and generating code. A team is often struggling with changing requirements and difficult technology. The team may not have built any functionality yet, but instead has tried to deliver requirements documents or business models. A development environment already exists and the team is familiar with the targeted technology.

In this case, I start by conducting Daily Scrums as the Scrum Master. I want to find out what is impeding the team. I may let these initial Daily Scrum meetings go on for hours. The team talks out its problems, including why it can't build software and how frustrated it is. I then challenge the team: "What can you build in the next thirty days?" I want to see the team work together to build something, to prove that it can develop software. I try to get the team to focus on functionality that is important to the customer. What really impresses the customer, though, is that the team can build something at all within thirty days. In many instances, the team has gone for months without producing any functionality and the customer has given up. My most immediate goal is to get the team to believe in itself, and to get the customer to believe in the team. The Sprint Goal is:

"Demonstrate any piece of user functionality on the selected technology."

At the Daily Scrums, I identify other impediments to the team's progress and help to remove them. If the team is able to build functionality during the first Sprint, the customer and team collaboratively determine what to do next at the Sprint Review and Sprint Planning meeting. I have never had a team fail to meet this challenge.

4.1.3   Improving Engineering Practices

As I implement Scrum, I evaluate the engineering practices that the team employs. Sometimes they are fine, sometimes they hinder the team, and sometimes they are missing. I use the Daily Scrum to identify any deficiencies. I then work with the team and management to improve them.

If an engineer reports in a Daily Scrum that he or she is working on a model, I might meet with the entire team after the meeting to discuss modeling practices. Is the team building models to guide its thinking about how to structure the code? Or is the team building models because it's been told that it has to build models before coding? If modeling is an existing practice, I might then discuss with engineering management whether the team can make modeling optional for this project. We'll have a discussion about the value of models as documentation, particularly since models go out of date as the system evolves. Keeping models synchronized with code is a maintenance burden on any organization. I usually recommend that management adopt a more "agile" practice, such as the one recommended by Scott Ambler (http://www.extreme-modeling.com/). I advocate an empirical approach in my discussions with management. Does the team become more productive if models are optional? If yes, then the team only uses models to guide their thinking. Does the code quality suffer if models are only used to guide thinking? If yes, then modeling is required where more rigor is needed.

If the team doesn't report any problems with the daily build at the Daily Scrum, I inquire why not. Daily builds always have problems. I sometimes find out that there is no daily build process. I view the absence of a daily build as dangerous. Without it, the team isn't required to synchronize its code. Without the daily build, the team might not know that the code doesn't compile cleanly. Without the daily build, there is no way to test the product daily. The team doesn't even know if the code holds together. If the team doesn't perform daily builds and tests, the team may have made less progress than it thinks. The daily build ensures that the team moves forward from a sound base every day.

As Scrum Master, I make judgments on a team's engineering practices (or lack of practices). The best Scrum Masters are also good engineers. The Scrum Master helps the team improve its engineering practices, just as a coach teaches a team to play better. He or she causes the team to reevaluate and discard wasteful practices, and to assess, design and adopt new practices. For instance, Mike Beedle likes many Extreme Programming practices. He has helped Scrum teams implement them within their projects.

4.2   Business Value through Collaboration

In this section, the term "management" refers interchangeably to the users, customers, or investors who fund the development projects.   —

Some people read about Scrum and think that it's a cop out. They think:

"Since everything is empirical, teams can reduce functionality or increase costs in order to meet goals! The system isn't even a fixed thing since the Product Backlog keeps emerging and evolving. How do I know what to expect, how do I stop the project from slipping and going out of control? How do I stop the team from slacking off, from letting the organization and the customer down? I want to be able to set a date and a cost. Then I'll hold the team responsible for delivering. If the team can't deliver, I'll contract to someone who can! This Scrum stuff doesn't provide me with adequate controls!"

These fears arise when someone doesn't know Scrum controls a project through active management involvement. The traditional approach to systems development begins by defining the system vision and overall requirements. The development organization (or external contractor) estimates the cost, and the expense of the system is budgeted. The system is developed and implemented. The customer expects the system to deliver the business value he or she envisioned, but often this expectation can't be verified for months after implementation. This is the "over the wall" approach to system development because there is little interaction between customer and development team.

Scrum requires much more collaboration between management, the customer, and the development team. The customer, aided by the team, still builds a vision and system requirements (Product Backlog). The myth that requirements can be definitively stated at the beginning of a project is dropped, however. A small set of high-priority requirements is stated initially, usually enough for three months of Sprints; the rest of the requirements emerge as the product emerges. The team prepares estimates and the customer allocates a budget for the initially foreseeable Product Backlog.

The team then develops new business functionality in thirty-day increments, or Sprints. At the end of each Sprint, management and the team review the functionality and consider its value. Is the cost of the functionality justified? Is development progressing as predicted? Are costs spiraling, and, if so, what can be done about it? Will the organization attain business value from the functionality that was demonstrated? Given what functionality has been developed so far, what should be developed next? Scrum provides management with direct control of the project at least every thirty days.

At the end of the first three Sprints, management is usually so pleased with the progress and the functionality already delivered that they budget for more functionality. Management looks at the Product Backlog and determines what they want to budget. If they want to budget for six months of functionality, they simply project the cost of the last Sprint over the next six months. The team(s) will continue to deliver functionality as long as the customer funds the development.

In my experience, Scrum teams deliver. I've mentioned that a Scrum team can reduce functionality to meet a Sprint Goal. However, I should note that the opposite is usually the case. Scrum lets the team find creative ways to meet their commitments. Teams usually rise to the occasion, take their commitments to heart, and surprise management at the Sprint Review by demonstrating more than they initially committed. Teams excel in the environment that Scrum provides. They usually do better than even they had estimated.

Management sometimes struggles with letting go of the planned, defined approach. Managers are used to defining everything at the beginning of a project and contracting a fixed price, fixed date with a team. This illusion of predictability is very reassuring and not easily cast aside. This illusion removes flexibility from the equation, though. Scrum asks management and customers to work with the Scrum team to create business value. Often, managers are only willing to give up their old bad habits when they experience the increased productivity and flexibility of Scrum. To others, the current situation is so bad they are willing to try anything that makes sense.

In the next section, I discuss how to manage empirically, using Scrum to maximize business value. I show how to measure the work planned for a release, to determine how quickly the work is being completed, and to estimate when the work will be done. More importantly, I show how to adapt to the realities of the work, adjusting costs, functionality, dates, and quality to meet an organization's requirements and maximize business value.

Projects are complex, unpredictable affairs, and management should always expect the unexpected. I'll discuss how to collaborate and make tradeoffs as a project proceeds. I'll show how to manage such questions as, "If I want more functionality in the release, what is the new probable release date given the team's productivity?" and "If I want an earlier release date, what functionality can I exclude given the team's productivity?"

Before we dive into the details of how to empirically manage a project, let's see what the experience feels like. Let's look at a project that lasts months rather than years and can be completed with one team. Let's see what it feels like for a first-time Scrum manager to manage empirically in a classic business environment.

4.2.1   Example of Scrum Management

Say you are the project manager for a rewrite of a system to implement new security and privacy capabilities. You are scheduled to appear before the Executive Committee to present the project and secure adequate funding and quality staff for it. The Executive Committee has never heard of Scrum before and is probably expecting that you have everything planned out on a pert chart. In preparation for the project, you draft a Product Backlog, tentatively select a team, prepare a budget, and identify a probable completion date.

Your **Product Backlog** lists the major pieces of work and requirements for the project. The team will have to identify security and privacy requirements, select appropriate products, open up and implement the products within the system, and test the system to ensure that it meets the security and privacy standards. You've detailed what has to be done and solicited the potential team's opinion in order to get accurate estimates of how much work each item entails. The estimates are the number of days that you think that the team you've selected will take to address and turn each backlog item into an updated system. You've brought in a security consultant from one of the vendors to review and revise your estimates. In short, you feel confident that you know what you're talking about.

The **Scrum Team** that you've selected consists of engineers who are familiar with the system and the best testers that you can find. You've also identified a consultant who knows the security and privacy regulations completely and has implemented several solutions previously. You've spoken with management and with other project managers to get the people on your team freed of other assignments if you get the go-ahead. All of your Product Backlog estimates are based on having this team assigned to the project.

The **project budget** consists of the costs for the team, consultant costs, travel costs, overhead, the cost of some new servers for development and testing, vendor software costs, and the cost of converting space into a Scrum Team room.

The **completion date** has been determined by adding up the work in the Product Backlog and dividing it by the amount of work that the team can accomplish every Sprint. You've assumed that everyone on the team is available eighteen days per month, having assessed everyone's vacation schedules and made some reasonable assumptions about sick time.

It's time to present to the Executive Committee. You discuss the project requirements and show how they are formatted in a prioritized Product Backlog. You discuss that this is a pretty complex project since it implements some not-yet-selected security and privacy software into existing systems. More complexity may occur as your team opens up the code because the code quality and clarity is suspect. A team has been identified with domain knowledge and you've added a consultant with specific security skills. You indicate to the Executive Committee that this project has enough complexity that you will be using a new development process called Scrum. You don't elaborate or make a big deal of Scrum, simply indicating that it will give you and the team the flexibility needed to handle the project's complexity. Scrum will let you and management collaborate monthly to keep on top of things and respond to unexpected problems promptly. You request that the Executive Committee appoint a Steering Committee for this monthly collaboration and for ongoing guidance.

You then present your project plan using a graph (see Figure 4.1, Project Plan). The graph indicates that the project will be complete within eight months. The Y-axis shows the estimated hours of Product Backlog work. The X-axis shows the number of months the project continues. The line shows a regular decrease in the estimated remaining work over the project's lifetime. In the eighth month, no work remains and the project is complete.

You intend to be done in eight months. Nonetheless, you warn the Executive Committee that estimating the duration of a project can be pretty complicated, and you promise to keep them apprised of your progress at each monthly meeting with the Steering Committee. There's some grumbling: some members of the Executive Committee want to know why you can't tell them precisely when you'll be done, just like the other project managers have. You discuss with them the complexity of the technology and requirements. You indicate that there's going to be a lot of learning on this project, that it contains a lot of research as well as development. You indicate that you can't guarantee an exact completion date because of these uncertainties and complexities, but that you will collaborate with the Steering Committee on a monthly basis. You, the team, and they will

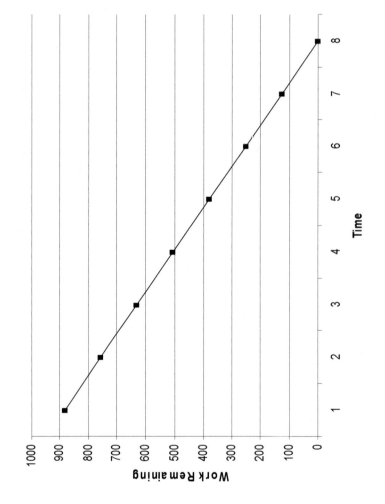

FIGURE 4.1: Project Plan

empirically determine the next best steps every thirty days to ensure that business value is maximized.

During the first Sprint, the team has to spend more time setting up the project environment than anticipated. The servers arrive late, and the development software has to be upgraded to work on the new operating system release. As a result, the team was able to complete less of the Product Backlog than planned. At the Sprint Review, the team demonstrates some initial security capabilities built into an existing business function. The functionality is a little less than the team had hoped to have completed, but it still demonstrates how the security functionality will work. You then review a revised project plan with the Steering Committee (see Figure 4.2, Project Plan with first correction).

This plan shows that the team was unable to complete as much Product Backlog as it had anticipated during the first month. Unless the Steering Committee wants to change the degree of security to be implemented or the scope of functionality to be addressed, the project right now looks like it will be complete approximately two weeks later than anticipated. The project looks like it will have two more weeks of cost. You are collaborating with the Steering Committee about what to do based on what you've found to date.

What you've presented to the Steering Committee is often called a "slip." Slip is a negative word, reflecting that the team didn't know what it was doing. Exactly right! The team was unable to estimate and predict everything that happened during the Sprint. An unexpected thing happened! This unexpected thing caused a two-week "slip." In complex technology projects with emerging requirements, you should expect the unexpected. Scrum provides you with direct, immediate visibility into the slip at least every thirty days. At that time, management and the team can collaborate on what should be done next, given the new reality. Every thirty days corrective action can be taken, rather than waiting for milestones or the end of the project. In this case, the Steering Committee directs you to continue as projected. They want to see what will happen during the next thirty days.

During the second Sprint, the team was able to accomplish more than anticipated. A vendor was selected and its security product was implemented into some of the system. The product simplifies the work that you had anticipated, so the team was able to easily replace and extend the security it built into the system during the last Sprint. The team has worked with you to re-estimate the product backlog. The new project plan that you present to the Steering Committee at the Sprint Review is shown in Figure 4.3, Project Plan with second correction.

Figure 4.3, Project Plan, shows that the team was able to find a solution that reduces the overall work estimated for the project. As a result,

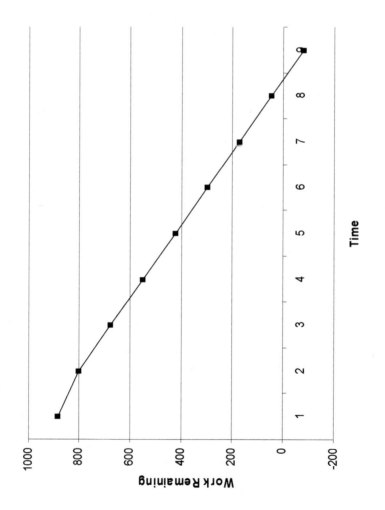

FIGURE 4.2: Project Plan with first correction

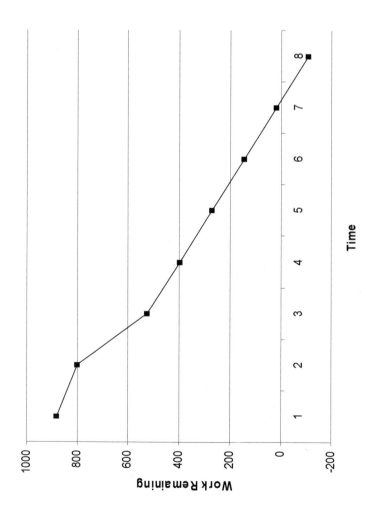

FIGURE 4.3: Project Plan with second correction

you now estimate that the project will be complete three weeks earlier than anticipated[1]. The Steering Committee is now starting to understand empirical management. It is seeing what is really happening every month and making appropriate decisions. The Steering Committee is able to guide the project month-by-month based on results, not promises. Consequently, it is glad that it didn't change anything the prior month.

The members of the Steering Committee were pleased to get to hear from the Scrum team directly and see some of the new product implemented. One Scrum team member demonstrated an attempted security breach and how the new software responded. This led to a discussion about the types of breaches that the project anticipates. The Steering Committee again directs you to proceed, and also asks you where the Daily Scrum meeting is held. They want to look in and see what's happening.

4.3   Empirical Management

Throw out the pert charts, because Scrum requires much less tedious but much more involved management action.

Management that employs Scrum is like a coach at the rugby or soccer game. It does everything possible to help the team play its best. It watches the team, makes substitutions, gets water, shouts advice, and cares passionately about the team and the game. The project is constantly changing. The activities within the project are constantly changing. Management watches while the game evolves and tries to help, but the game is in the team's hands (or feet).

As management watches a Sprint evolve, it is assessing progress and making decisions about how to help the team be more productive and how to help the team cope with what it is encountering. If a team is struggling with technology far more complicated than initially envisioned, management thinks about what would help. Is training helpful? Would a consultant be useful? Should the technology be replaced? Management studies the team during the Sprint. Between Sprints, management works with the team to make adjustments that make the next Sprint better. All of the changes result from direct observation.

Scrum demands the liberal application of common sense. If the date can't be met, reduce the functionality that will be delivered. If the functionality can't be reduced, reduce some of the capabilities within the functionality. Increase the cost by adding another team that Sprints in parallel, or bring in experts. Scrum will put all of the information that is needed to make these decisions at management's fingertips. Management then has to decide how to maximize business value from the project.

---

[1] The security product is so powerful and easy to use that you suspect all the remaining work will be easier than anticipated. However, you want to get another Sprint of experience before changing the estimates.

FIGURE 4.4: Observations

Management is primarily responsible for doing anything possible to increase team productivity and then adapting to the results. Management should live and breathe to help the teams. Nothing is more important. If the team needs meeting rooms, executives can do nothing better than move out of their corner offices to make sure the team keeps charging ahead.

Scrum provides two types of information to management: **first-hand observations** (see Figure 4.4, Observations), and **backlog graphs** charts. Management must actively, intelligently use these to stay on top of the project and make decisions. There is no place for hands-off management with Scrum.

4.3.1   Use Frequent, First-Hand Observations

Scrum provides direct visibility into the progress of the project.

Daily Scrums provide a direct view into each team's progress. Management attends and observes team spirit, each member's participation, team member interaction, work that is being completed, decisions that need to be made, and impediments that need to be removed.

Listen closely at the Daily Scrum to what is being said as well as how it is being said. If a team member is discouraged, find out why. How can he or she rearrange the work or get help to make more progress? If most of the team seems to be floundering, what are they having trouble with?

What expertise can be brought to bear? Meet with the team afterwards and talk through its problems. If you hear conflicting approaches to a design, gather the individuals afterwards and talk through the design. If a team member hasn't been to a Scrum for several days, where is he or she? How can you bring him or her back to work? Is he or she at an unnecessary organizational meeting? Listen closely and see what you can do to help the team. The team will do the best it can do. You monitor what is happening and see how you can help it communicate better, organize better, go around obstacles, and be more productive.

At Sprint Reviews, the Scrum Team demonstrates to management what it has been able to produce. The team demonstrates the real, executable product functionality that it has built. Maybe the team has also developed models, designs, architectures, and use cases. These artifacts are only useful to the degree that they've guided team thinking. What really matters is the product functionality delivered. You can't ship a design. You can ship working code.

During the Sprint Review, the team discusses what happened during the Sprint. What problems did it encounter with the technology? What alternate approaches and designs did it use? What contradictions did it find in the requirements? To what degree was it able to meet the Sprint goal? To what depth is the product functionality implemented? How well tested is the code? How stable of a base does the product increment represent for the future? How well is the team working together? What other expertise could it use?

These questions are fodder for management action. Carefully listening to the team helps you formulate better decisions. How should you change the team composition, if at all? Does the team need to do more technology, infrastructure, environment, or design work in the next Sprint? Does the next Sprint need to deepen already implemented functionality, or start adding new functionality? At the end of the Sprint, you are provided the best available information to make these decisions. You can now effectively help the team prepare for the next Sprint.

4.3.2   Backlog, Assessing Progress and Predicting the Future

Management sets objectives. Management then reports progress towards meeting these objectives. We had planned for this release by the end of the third quarter; will it be ready? Management needs to be able to answer questions about:

Sprint progress – how is the team progressing toward its Sprint goal?

Release progress – when will the release be ready with the quality and functionality desired? Do changes need to be made to the release to get it by a certain date? Do additional resources need to be added to get the release on time with the needed functionality?

Product progress – how is the product filling out compared to what's needed in the marketplace?

First hand observations provide part of the answer to these questions. The work backlog provides the rest of the answer. Work backlog is the amount of work remaining to be done at any point in time. Backlog trends can be derived by plotting estimated work remaining in backlog across time. The backlog trend indicates the team's ability to decrease its backlog. Backlog trends will vary by team and will vary across time. Variables such as team skills, backlog estimate accuracy, and unexpected complexities affect the trend line.

Work backlog and backlog trends can be assessed for a Sprint and for a product release. Less reliably, backlog and trends can be assessed for a product or an entire system, delivered in multiple releases.

Sprint Backlog consists of the tasks that the Scrum Team has devised for a Sprint. These tasks are work to transform the selected Product Backlog into the Sprint goal. They are estimated in hours, usually ranging from four to sixteen hours of work each. At the Sprint Planning meeting, the team constructs this backlog and estimates the amount of time to complete each backlog item. The team might use dependency diagrams to ensure that they've figured out all of the work. As a team member works on a Sprint backlog item, he or she is responsible for updating the estimate of the remaining hours to complete that work. This estimate may go up if the work is more complicated than initially estimated. The estimate may have been too high, so less work is required than anticipated. Regardless, once a task is started, the team members doing the work update this estimate daily until the backlog item is completed and work remaining is zero.

Unanticipated work is often discovered and uncovered by the team as it builds the product increment. The team is responsible for creating new backlog items for this work and estimating the work to complete each of them.

Release Backlog is that subset of Product Backlog that is selected for a release. The Product Backlog list is all work that is known for a product. Starting at the highest priority work, the Product Owner segments this work into probable releases. The first seventy-two Product Backlog items are targeted for a Release 11.2 due in the third quarter of 2001. The seventy-third to one hundred sixtieth Product Backlog items are targeted for a Release 11.3 due in the first quarter of 2002. As the Scrum teams build product during each Sprint, the Product Owner may empirically adjust the Product Backlog planned for each release. If more work is getting done than expected, the Product Owner may opt for an earlier release date, or a release with some of the functionality initially planned for Release 11.3.

Each Product Backlog item has an estimate that was entered by the Product Owner. Release backlog is estimated in days. The Product Owner is responsible for describing the Product Backlog items and working with the team to reach the best possible estimates. The Product Owner revises these estimates when more details regarding each item become available.

Product Backlog consists of all work that can be foreseen for a product. Backlog consists of product features, functionality, infrastructure, architecture, and technology work. The Product Owner estimates the amount of work in days to implement each item. Product backlog that is not included in the next product release tends to be of less interest to management and the Product Owner. This Product Backlog usually is less precisely described and estimated than the backlog for the next release. Predictions based on the estimates for these backlog items tend to be less reliable than release estimates because the Product Backlog contains many lower priority items that would be nice to have but may never be implemented. The owner of the Product Backlog is responsible for keeping these estimates up-to-date as best as possible.

4.4   Managing a Sprint

Managing a Sprint means helping the team to meet its Sprint goal. The team has selected the Product Backlog and established a Sprint goal. You help the team by removing impediments and making decisions. You can also help the team by monitoring its work and progress toward completion. If the team doesn't appear able to complete all of its work, you can help it reassess how it can reduce the work and still meet the Sprint goal. If this is impossible, you can work with it to consider canceling and reformulating the Sprint. As you and the team work together, you will get better at establishing and meeting Sprint goals.

The team constructed the Sprint Backlog and keeps it updated. The Sprint Backlog is all of the work that the team identifies as necessary to meet the Sprint goal. You can help the team track the progress through the Sprint Backlog graph.

To create this graph, determine how much work remains by summing the backlog estimates every day of the Sprint. The amount of work remaining for a Sprint is the sum of the work remaining for all of the Sprint Backlog. Keep track of these sums by day and use them to create a graph that shows the work remaining over time. By drawing a line through the points on the graph, you can identify a team's progress in completing a Sprint's work.

A friend of mine asked, "The estimates are of effort, the mapping is against time. How do you determine duration from effort if the tasks have no preordained sequence?" This question indicates the difficulty shifting from a pert chart-based, time reporting structure to an empirical approach. Duration is not considered in Scrum. Work remaining and date are the only variables of interest, with work remaining managed to reach zero by the end of the Sprint.

Figure 4.5, Perfect Backlog Graph, is an example of a suspiciously perfect Sprint's backlog graph.

Figure 4.5 shows a Sprint finishing with zero work remaining. The work remaining line descends linearly from 1680 hours to zero hours over the thirty day Sprint, declining by 56 hours of work per day. All the tasks were completed according to initial estimate, the team worked regularly the same amount each day with everyone at work, and no new work or shortcuts were uncovered.

If you ever see a Sprint Backlog trend graph like the above, be wary. For a graph like this to reflect reality, the team had to prepare a perfect Sprint Backlog during the Sprint Planning meeting. No additional work was required, and no work had to be removed. The team also updated the Sprint Backlog estimates every day, reducing the estimates on all tasks by 56 hours. The likelihood of this happening approaches zero. Compare the graph to what you've been hearing in the Daily Scrums. No team can ever be this good and this methodical. For instance, this graph shows that the team is reducing the amount of work 56 hours per day, every day. Does this mean that the team works Saturday and Sunday as well as work days? That's what the graph says!

Figure 4.6, More Likely Backlog Graph, is a much more likely backlog chart for a Sprint.

In Figure 4.6, the diamonds represent the sum of estimated work remaining for all Sprint Backlog for each day. A line connecting the diamonds tracks estimated work remaining across a Sprint. As you manage Sprints, you will learn to interpret these graphs. There are general interpretations, and specific patterns that you will find for your teams.

In the Sprint graphed above, what actually happened is described in Table 1, Sprint Signature Description.

The team was in a time-box, a Sprint of thirty days. On day 18, the team had too much functionality to complete by the end of the Sprint. The team met with the Product Owner and Scrum Master to assess if it could still meet the Sprint Goal with some work removed or some functionality implemented with less detail. Some work was removed and the team proceeded to meet the Sprint Goal within thirty days.

Work remaining reporting updates the estimated number of hours required to complete a task. **This should not be confused with time reporting, which is not part of Scrum. There are no mechanisms in Scrum for tracking the amount of time that a team works. Teams are measured by meeting goals, not by how many hours they take to meet the goal. Scrum is result oriented, not process oriented.**

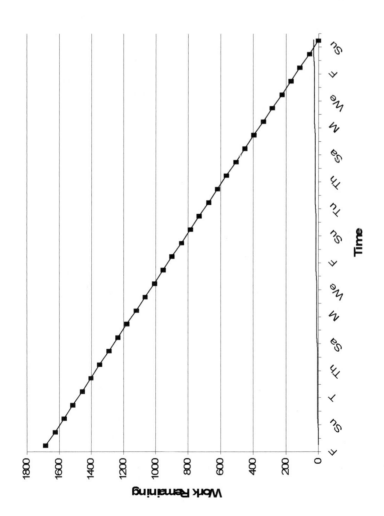

FIGURE 4.5: Perfect Backlog Graph

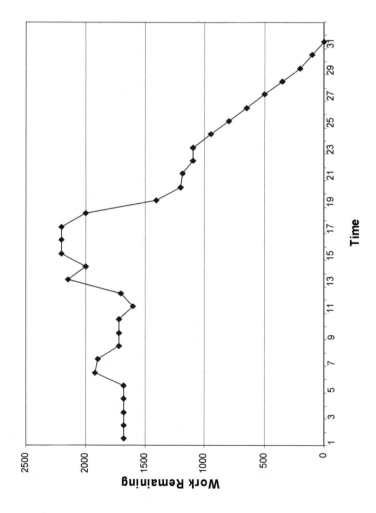

FIGURE 4.6: More Likely Backlog Graph

4.4.1   Sprint Signatures

As a team works together, it develops its own style of creating and maintaining the Sprint Backlog. It also demonstrates unique work patterns; some teams working consistently, some in bursts, some at the end of a Sprint. Some teams seek pressure, while others seek regularity. Across time, the backlog charts of each team develop predictable patterns. They stabilize as the team learns the technology, the business or product domain, and each other. These chart patterns are called Sprint signatures. When you graph how a team works, you see its signature. The signature should be a reflection – another validation – of what you hear in the daily Scum meeting. Once a team settles into a signature, watch for changes. Just like a person changes their signature when stressed, so does a team. Signature changes are another source of information to help manage a team.

For instance, some teams always have Sprint Backlog that keeps going up during the first part of the Sprint, and then descends dramatically. Assess the measurements and determine whether this is because of inadequate Sprint planning, overwork during the last ten days (which usually causes poor quality), or infrequent estimation of work remaining. Let's look at some signatures and interpret what they might mean.

Whenever the estimated hours remain the same from day to day, the team isn't updating its estimates as it works (or, less likely, no one worked). Figure 4.7, Sprint signature, shows this happening. You will see this type of signature from newer Scrum teams. During the first ten days, the team apparently forgot to update the Sprint Backlog with new estimates. On the eleventh day, it was reminded of this responsibility. It updated the estimates, which on the twelfth day reflected 1100 estimated hours of work remaining. The team had similar problems estimating the Sprint Backlog from the 15th to 25th day. Management and the Scrum Master can't use this graph to help them understand what's going on in the Sprint, or what they can do to help. Until the Scrum Master gets the team to update the Sprint Backlog as it works, management will have to rely on observations during the Daily Scrum to get information.

Figure 4.8, Sprint signature for underestimating, is classic for a new Scrum team. The team is learning to work together as well as learning the technology, the development environment, and/or the domain. Its estimating skills aren't that good yet. The team has their Sprint Planning meeting on the first day and estimates 1680 hours of work in the Sprint Backlog. The team then goes home for the weekend. On the first week of work, the team re-estimates Sprint Backlog as it works on it. Each day, the estimated remaining hours increase as the team discovers new work and revises estimates upward for existing work. The team again goes home for the weekend on the 9th and 10th days. During the next week, including the weekend, the team makes a concerted effort and gets a lot of work done.

Period	Event
Day 1	Sprint planning meeting, Sprint Backlog established with a 1680 estimated hours of work.
Days 2-3	Weekend days, no work done and no changes in estimated work remaining.
Days 4-5	The team worked but didn't adjust the estimated work remaining figures on their tasks. The estimated work remaining didn't show a drop because of this neglect.
Days 6-8	The team started adjusting estimated work remaining figures on tasks. On day 6, the estimates showed more work. Then work remaining declined.
Days 9-10	Weekend days, no work done and no changes in estimated work remaining.
Day 11	Some work done by the team and the estimated work remaining declined.
Days 12-15	The team discovered that some more tasks were required and that some of the tasks it was working on would take more time than first estimated. Estimated time remaining jumps to 2150 hours.
Days 16-17	The team is discouraged by all of the work remaining and didn't work during the weekend. No changes in estimated time remaining.
Day 18	The team works more and its remaining work declined. The team then met with the Product Owner and the Scrum Master to determine what tasks could be reduced or removed while still meeting the goals of the Sprint. Some Sprint Backlog was dropped; other estimates were lowered because not as much functionality had to be supported. Overall estimated work remaining reduced to 1400 hours. If all of this work is completed, the team will still meet the Sprint Goal, although with functionality implemented less completely.
Day 19	The team continues work toward the Sprint Goal using new Sprint Backlog. Estimated work remaining declines.
Days 20-30	Team is motivated because it can still meet the Sprint Goal if it works hard. The team works regularly including during the weekends. Estimated work remaining declines to zero as the team meets its Sprint Goal by the 31st day.

TABLE 4.1: Sprint signature description

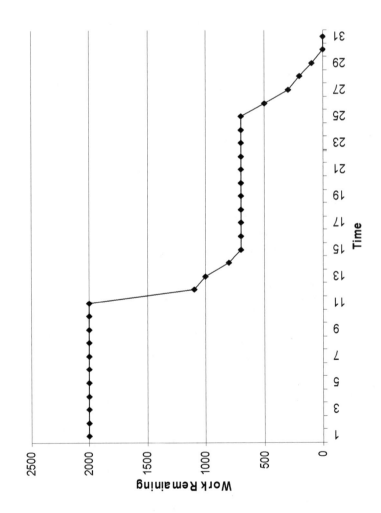

FIGURE 4.7: Sprint signature

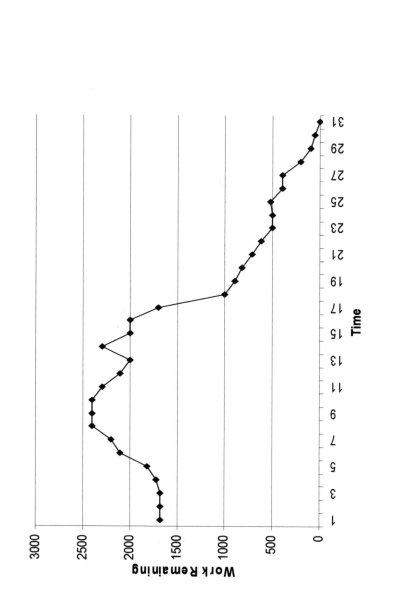

FIGURE 4.8: Sprint signature for underestimating

The estimated remaining work is down to 1700 hours by the end of the 17th day, Sunday. On the 18th day, the team is discouraged that it will not get all of the work done by the end of the Sprint, so the team meets with the Scrum Master, project manager, and Product Owner. Collectively, they figure out how they can lessen the depth of the functionality and still meet the Sprint goals. They remove about 700 hours of work from the Sprint Backlog, reducing the estimated remaining work to 1000 hours. The team then works steadily to complete the Sprint. This team will be more careful in its estimates for the next Sprint, which should be easier since it is more experienced in the domain, technology, and collaboration using Scrum.

In Figure 4.9, Sprint signature for overestimating, a Scrum team makes its initial estimate and begins working after the weekend. At the end of every day, the work remaining is far less than it had expected. The team was unsure of the technology and the domain. As a result, it consistently overestimated the work. By the 11th day, the Scrum team realizes that it is going to be done well before the end of the Sprint on the 30th day. On the 12th, the team meets with the Scrum Master, project manager and Product Owner. The team could complete the product increment and close out the Sprint early (the trend line indicates zero work remaining on about the 17th day). Or, the team can deepen the degree to which it is implementing the functionality, building in more design and architecture. The team has its teeth into the work and recommends that it be allowed to take on more work. Everyone concurs. The team continues and successfully closes out the Sprint with more and deeper functionality than it had initially estimated.

As I've monitored backlog trends, I've found that teams tend to go from one signature type to another as they learn the domain, tools, Scrum, and as they self-organize. After three or four Sprints, however, a team tends to stabilize around a signature that characterizes its collective personality: risk takers, cautious, methodical, or over timers. Once the team starts updating the work remaining figures regularly, I've found that the signature reflects what I see daily in the Scrum meetings.

4.5   Managing a Release

The product is released to meet customer or marketplace obligations. The release balances functionality, cost, and quality requirements against date commitments.

I first presented Scrum at OOPSLA'96. The presentation was followed by some heated discussion. I had emphasized the empirical nature of Scrum, where management trades off cost, functionality, time, and quality as work progresses and more is known about requirements and the technology. The most heated criticism was, "I have to tell my management exactly what it's going to get, what the budget is, and when I'll deliver.

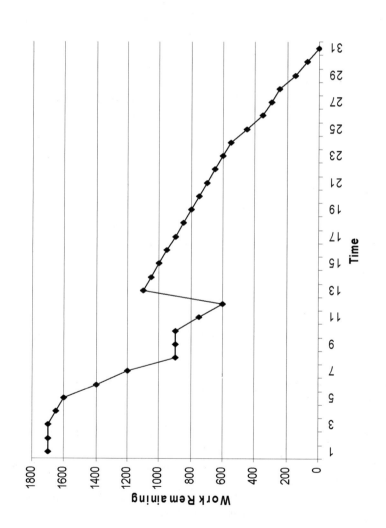

FIGURE 4.9: Sprint signature for overestimating

My management expects that from me." Another attendee was the product manager at a large software company. He had to annually present the release plan to the board, and he didn't want to tell them that cost, functionality, time and quality would have to be varied empirically as the release was worked on. He said, "My board would fire me if I presented that to them."

Scrum provides an alternate way to work with the management and board of directors. For example, Jeff Sutherland, VP of Engineering, went to the President of Easel Corporation, and asked him, "Have you ever seen a development team meet a traditional project plan." He said, "No." Jeff said, "I think the only thing you can trust is working software that the team can demo. If you give the team complete freedom for 30 day Sprints, at the end of the Sprint you will see exactly where the product is, for better or worse." He said, "Fine, for the first time I will know where product development really stands and can make the appropriate decisions. I'm willing to take the risk of giving the team autonomy for defined periods."

These comments reflect a dilemma in the software industry. We systems professionals know that tradeoffs have to be made, that everything can't be known in advance. Our management wants predictability. We usually wind up telling our management what they want to hear. Is that so bad? Management doesn't know, and it pretty much gets what we said, unless a real catastrophe occurs. What we lose is our management's participation, knowledge, guidance, and wisdom. If management understood that we were making tradeoffs, it could participate and collaborate. There would be no surprises. By telling management that we can deliver exactly what we say, we're setting management up for the big surprise.

4.5.1   Manage Cost, Date, Quality and Functionality

The customer is paying for the product. The product isn't a fixed entity. It's a tradeoff between the money the customer wants to spend, the business value that they want to get for the money, the date on which they feel they need the product, and the expected quality. Anyone who has had a house built for them knows this type of negotiation. They know that the negotiation doesn't just happen at the start of the job, it happens throughout the job. Building software is a lot more unpredictable than building a house.

Management's job is to manage the four variables of cost, date, functionality, and quality as development proceeds. Management helps the customer tradeoff one variable against another, while still meeting their objectives. Sometimes management and the team can deliver on all four variables. More often, management has to intelligently and openly negotiate and make tradeoffs between the four variables with the customers.

While discussing the four variables with customers, don't hide anything. I've seen products promised for a date when the project manager already knew he or she would have to deliver shallower functionality or provide a product that wasn't stable. But the project manager didn't want to disappoint the customer, so he or she agreed to the date without disclosing the reduced functionality and quality. Excruciating honesty, sharing what we know and believe, is best. Then we can work closely with the customer during development based on what's really happening, not spend time trying to cover up. **Establishing an open, honest relationship with the customer is the most important aspect of Scrum; Scrum makes everything visible; it's real hard to cover up incorrect expectations that you established with the customer.**

4.5.2   Basis for Tradeoffs

The product backlog graph is the quantitative tool for making tradeoffs between cost, time, functionality and quality for a release. This graph tracks the estimated days of work remaining through a release. Each product backlog item contains its amount of estimated work remaining. The Product Owner updates these values weekly. The graph uses the y-axis for the estimated work remaining, and the x-axis for the project or release time scale. Plot the sum of estimated days remaining on that date. Keep track of these plots across time. Even though you might think that backlog should always go down, new work is always being discovered as the product is being built. Expect the backlog to go up and down.

A release that is going just the way you expected, with a release in week 20, is shown in Figure 4.10, Excellent Release Control.

There is too much complexity and too many variables in even the simplest project for Figure 4.10 to ever occur. Figure 4.10 implies that the Product Owner was able to predict everything the product would require prior to the project beginning. No additional functionality was added during the release, or if functionality was added an exact amount of other functionality was removed. The graph also implies that the Sprint team was able to regularly and systematically proceed with development on this system without any surprises or unexpected complexities.

More likely you will graph a backlog chart over the course of a project that looks like Figure 4.11, Release with reduced functionality.

The Product Owner initially estimated 5400 hours of work for the system to be completed and released on the 20th month. Two Scrum Teams were established and assigned to the project. This graph looks like the Product Owner started getting worried about the seventh month. The Product Backlog was not being reduced quickly enough for the release to occur on the 20th month. Perhaps coordinating the number of Scrum teams was harder than anticipated. Perhaps the domain was hard for the

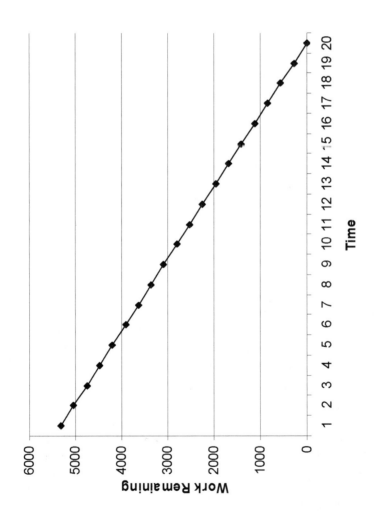

FIGURE 4.10: Excellent Release Control

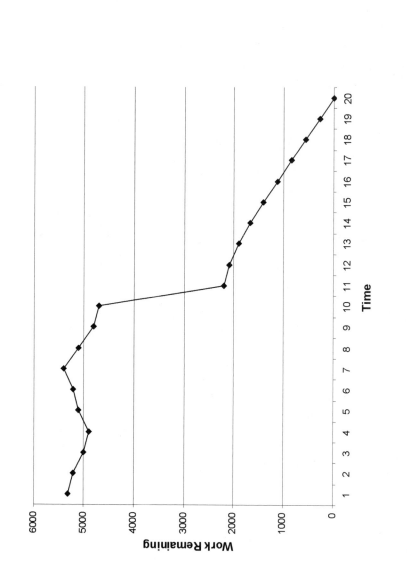

FIGURE 4.11: Release with reduced functionality

developers to understand, the technology was difficult to get to work, or the functionality was underestimated. The backlog work was not decreasing on a slope that would meet the release date during the 20th month. To determine the work slope, or trend, draw a line representing average slope over a period of time. Project it to determine when no work is likely to be left. In Figure 4.11, the Product Owner and users needed the release by the 20th month. When they drew trend lines during months 8 and 9, their suspicion that there was too much work were confirmed. They met with the team and reassessed what functionality could be delivered to meet release objectives by the 20th month. As a result of the meeting, a number of functions were dropped from this release and others made shallower. Remaining Product Backlog dropped from 4800 to 2200 days. The project proceeded and the teams were able to meet the release date with the new functionality.

On some projects, management is able to increase the costs without changing the release date or functionality. One way to increase costs is to add teams to the project. The multiple teams work together in parallel on the same Product Backlog.

In Figure 4.12, Release with second team added, the Product Owner and management monitored the work trend for the first five months. They assessed that they were not going to meet the scheduled release date unless they changed something. They were proactive, and created and added a second team to the project. Since members of the second team were already familiar with the domain and technology, the second team was immediately productive. The result of adding the second team was more work done per month than initially planned. This was the selected alternative when more work than originally expected was discovered.

Figure 4.13, Release date slipped, shows another project where the Product Owner and management again assessed that the backlog wasn't dropping as quickly as had been expected. However, the product wasn't top priority, so they chose to let the release date slip. They plotted the trend line around the ninth month (when the team had stabilized) and projected a four-week slip. The customer agreed to the slip and the release date was changed.

Adjusting cost, time, quality, and functionality may have to be done more than once during a release if trends are not going as expected.

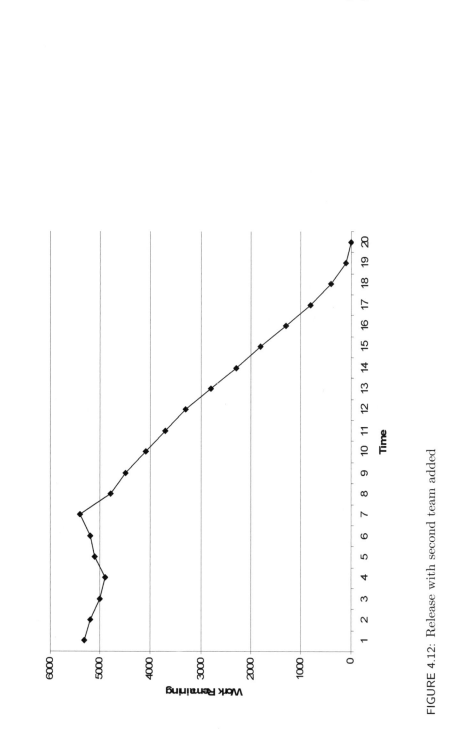

FIGURE 4.12: Release with second team added

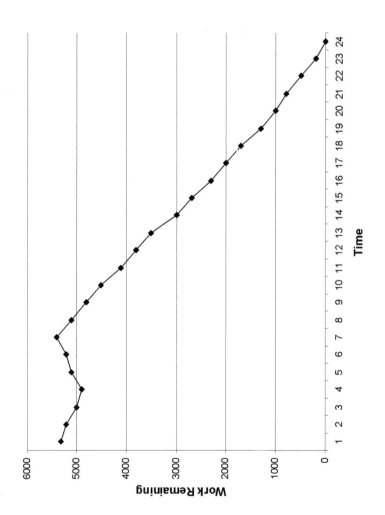

FIGURE 4.13: Release date slipped

CHAPTER 5

Why Scrum?

Scrum is built on an empirical process control model which is radically different from the defined model that most processes and methodologies use. This section provides the framework for Scrum. —

Why Scrum? presents the heart and soul of Scrum. Scrum is based on completely different assumptions and foundations than the current systems development methodologies. Scrum is based on an empirical process control model rather than the traditional defined process control model. This section shows why the empirical model is appropriate for systems development projects and the current defined model is not. Once you understand Scrum's empirical roots, you will be able to understand why Scrum looks and feels different, why it works, and how it is a true paradigm shift.

I introduced Individual, Inc. in Chapter 1, Introduction. The PNP team was unsuccessfully trying to develop a product in a very noisy, conflicting, complicated, frustrating environment. Everyone had the top priority feature to be built and needed it to be built now. Scrum allowed the team to cut through the noise and complexity. The team was able to focus for thirty day Sprints and build the product one increment at a time. In this section, I'll discuss the noise that teams such as the PNP team tried to work within. I'll discuss how this is common to all systems development projects, and I'll describe how Scrum solves the problem.

5.1 Noisy Life

In this context, the term "noise" refers not to a sonic phenomenon, but to the unpredictable, irregular, nonlinear parts of system development. Noise is the unanticipated part of any activity that disrupts the habits of a lifetime. Noise is what causes that unexpected glitch that requires my full attention. Noise is everywhere. Noise agitates the signals on my mobile phone so I have trouble understanding the other person. Noise distorts electricity traveling across power lines and causes my PC to shut down. My kids make noise and keep me from hearing my wife. When noise-to-signal ratio is too high, the sound of what I want to hear is obscured by the sound of what I don't want to hear, or the noise.

Even a really solid number like "0.00" starts displaying its noise when I look out past those first two decimal points. I can take a measure of the kitchen counter: it's 12 feet 4 inches. But I'd better be more precise, like 12.38 feet, because I need a fit without any gaps. But my measurement has noise from rounding. The space for the counter is really 12.374452 feet. And when I cut the counter, there will be more noise from the width of the saw blade. Noise, imprecision, uncertainty, unpredictability are everywhere.

Complexity theory can be seen as a whole new way of understanding the causes and patterns of noise. Noise, it turns out, is an inherent part of everything. It has always existed; rounding is a mechanism for ignoring it. Perfect, precise numbers are illusions that allow me to believe in predictability. If I assume that the length of my kitchen counter is 12.38 inches, and all the other noise being made is compatible with the noise of this length; I'll get away with glossing over the noise behind this number, and the counter will fit.

A great example of interference can be found on the American Psychological Association web site. You can find it on the cover of this book as Figure 5.1, Color Test. Don't read the words in the Color Test. Just say what color they're printed in out loud, as fast as you can. You're in for a surprise!

red

yellow

green

blue

red

blue

yellow

green

blue*l*

FIGURE 5.1: Color Test

If you're like most people, your first impulse was to read "red, yellow, green...," rather than the colors that the words are printed in – 'blue, green, red...' Noise has just interfered with your perception. When you look at one of the words, you see both its *color* and its *meaning*. If those two pieces of evidence are in conflict, you have to make a choice. Because experience has taught you that the meaning of a word is more important than the color of the word, interference occurs when you try to pay attention *only* to the ink color. The interference effect suggests you're not always in complete control of what you pay attention to. Noise interferes.

All physical processes exhibit some degree of noisy, or unpredictable, behavior. I've learned to selectively filter out noise, paying less attention to the predictable and more attention to the unpredictable. This focus on what really requires my immediate attention allows me to function in a very chaotic world.

5.2   Noise in Systems Development Projects

Systems development projects used to have much less noise. One of the first applications I ever built was an order entry system for Sears Roebuck & Company. Sears was automating the existing order entry process to improve efficiency. Since it wasn't reinventing the process, all I had to do was inspect what was already being done manually. I used assembler language to code the target application, which became one program in a job stream that ran daily on IBM System 360 computers. The IBM hardware, MVT operating system, assembler, and job control had been around for two years when I first started using them. When I had questions, I could turn to anyone in the department for answers. IBM manuals describing how the technologies worked were everywhere. There was very little noise in this systems development project. Almost everything was known and understood; I was the only unpredictable thing since I was a junior programmer.

During the 1980's and 1990's, systems started to be used for competitive advantage. Systems implemented wholly new processes or caused existing processes to be discerned in new ways (for instance, Internet banking). One technology followed another in rapid succession, many replacing their predecessors before they were thoroughly understood. For example, although many client server systems were deployed, the version control problems of sustaining multiple applications and dll's on multiple platforms and operating system releases were never mastered. Instead, the industry shifted to the thin-client, n-tier model, simplifying one problem while introducing a whole new set of challenges. I was recently at a board of directors meeting of a systems product company. One board member lamented, "Whatever happened to technology plateaus?"

Noise in systems development is a function of the three vectors of requirements, technology and people. If the product requirements are well known and the engineers know exactly how to build the requirements into a product using the selected technology, there is very little noise or unpredictability. The work proceeds linearly, in a straight line, with no false starts, little rework, and few mistakes. Noise increases as requirements are less understood and agreed upon. Noise increases as the ability to employ the selected technology is more uncertain. Development projects that build new processes on new technologies are very noisy and unpredictable.

The rollout of products based on new technology and functionality has accelerated. Certainty and reliability have been traded for competitive advantage. If too much time is spent thinking through requirements, competition gets to the market first. Products are both built into new technologies, and new technologies are used to build products! Building software for handheld operating systems that synchronize with object databases across wireless networks introduces enough new development and implementation platforms to make a sane person stagger.

For example, in the mid-1990's X-ray, CT Scan, and MRI pictures began to be generated in digital format rather than film. Healthcare institutions envisioned serving up these images on demand to radiologists as part of a workflow system. By applying Internet and Web technology, worldwide teams of radiologists could collaborate in real time. If the healthcare software company that I was working with could build systems to provide this functionality first, it would gain a significant competitive advantage.

One requirement was to serve up the digital image from a RAID 1 disk archive to the radiologist's workstation. This seemed pretty straight forward, and I expected a relatively predictable set of work for the team. As the team dug into the work, a whole raft of unexpected complications occurred. The radiologist's display could be either a high-resolution workstation or a regular computer monitor. The available bandwidth might be very high, or only 56kb. The radiologist needed to be able to rotate and zoom the images, and compare different images in a sequence so buffering might be required. A type of compression could be used to transmit images, but only if the degree of loss was within acceptable limits, such limits not having been yet formally defined. The FDA hadn't yet decided whether the display of these images was a medical device; if it were, a whole new set of testing and implementation requirements applied.

The development team was coping with new technologies, changing requirements, and a variety of implementation alternatives. It had to decide how to meld the technology and requirements into a demonstrable product in six months. Every time it dug into a piece of technology, new complications and difficulties arose. Every time it tried to finalize a require-

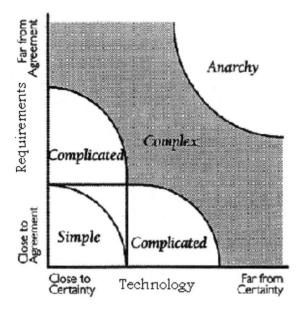

FIGURE 5.2: Project complexity. (From: Strategic Management and Organisational Dynamics The Challenge of Complexity—3rd Edition by Ralph D. Stacey, Financial Times, Harlow, England)

ment, new alternatives would be proposed. Both the requirements and the technology were unpredictable and so noisy that the team had trouble settling down and focusing on any one solution. Changing technology and requirements were making it hard for the team to focus and proceed.

Figure 5.2, Project complexity, is a graph that can be used to determine the noise level in any systems development project. On the y-axis, I plot the degree of uncertainty that exists about the project requirements. If project requirements are thoroughly understood, then noise will probably be low. If the requirements are only partially understood or are still emergent, then the noise level is likely to be high. On the x-axis, I plot the likelihood that the selected technologies will be able to help accomplish the project's goals. This is known as "technology certainty." If all of the technology is familiar and can be reliably implemented to achieve project goals, then the noise level is low. If the technology is emerging and has not been fully tested, the noise is high. For example, mainframe, batch system development is associated with simple, low noise projects. N-tier, web-deployed wireless technologies are associated with complicated or complex, high noise projects.

I haven't included the third vector, people, into the equation. When people are factored in, nothing is simple. The complexity of individuals and individuals working in teams raises the noise level for all projects. By factoring in people, I automatically increase a project's complexity category by one level. For instance, a project with certain technology and agreed upon functionality is now categorized as complicated rather than simple because of the people vector.

A project's noise category indicates what approach should be employed for managing the project and building the system. There are two approaches in process control theory to control and manage processes. The first model is called the **defined** process control model. When processes are simple with unobtrusive noise, I can write a definition of how they work and use this definition to repeat the processes over and over, each time generating the same results. These are called **defined processes**. Management and control is exercised by defining the processes so well that everything is known and predictable.

Management and control arise from the predictability of defined processes. Since the processes are defined, they can be grouped together and be expected to continue to operate predictably and repeatably. In such clusters of processes, the defined process control model can be used for modeling and controlling such simple systems as traffic lights, or such involved but defined systems as manufacturing pharmaceuticals. **Almost no systems development project is so simple, has so little noise, for the defined process control model to be appropriate by itself.**

If the process cannot be described in enough detail to be repeated, if there is so much complexity that any attempt to model the process results in different outcomes, the process is called a **complex process**. If I operate a complex process two times in a row, the results are more likely to be different than the same. The activities in the process are so noisy that their output cannot be predicted with an adequate degree of reliability. **Empirical** process control models are used to manage and control complex processes. Management and control is exercised through frequent inspection and adaptive response.

5.3   Why Current System Development Methodologies Don't Work

Most current system development methodologies claim that they can be used for a wide range of projects and system development efforts. The defined control and management model is employed by these methodologies. These methodologies contain a knowledge base of development processes and techniques. Every process and technique in the knowledge base is defined as though it were simple and repeatable. The knowledge base is threaded together by dependencies into defined project templates. Each template can be applied to a specific type of project, such as interface development, online development, and web development using object-oriented techniques. Since the processes and the relationships between them are defined, the companies purveying the methodologies claim that the templates can be used repeatedly for that type of project.

For the defined control mechanisms to work, these methodologies must define each process with enough accuracy that the resultant noise does not interfere with its repeatability, or the predictability of the outcome. I can watch engineers define a class numerous times and write down a definition of what I saw happening. This process definition is only useful if it can be repeated over and over to generate solid class descriptions. If my observations are general or loose because many variations are employed to derive a class, the process definition is useless. The process definition will be so weakly defined that, when it is employed, it does not generate repeatable results. When an activity is so complex or complicated that a different definition is required each time it is executed, the activity cannot be abstracted into a process definition.

All current systems development methodologies are based on partial and weak definitions of development activities. Methodologies often contain thousands of process definitions. I've evaluated process definitions in many major commercial methodologies. After lengthy inspection and analysis, I couldn't find a single process that was defined in enough detail to ensure repeatable outputs. For example, a process from one methodology described the resources to complete the process: 3.5 designers will complete a process within 16 hours if there are 4 classes. Classes to what level of functionality, with what interfaces, defined and built with what tools? What level of designers are these, with what skills in OO, and how do they feel that day? Without this level of definition, the process simply is not repeatable or predictable.

If I observe a class of activities that are simple and of relatively low noise, I can abstract them into a model that defines their behavior. This model defines the process operation in enough detail that I can then use it to guide and control future similar activities. Because I know what is going to happen, I can create a detailed description of it. Because noise is low, the project details can be used repeatedly with minimal disruption. The outcome of the activity is predictable.

Newton's laws are such an abstraction. Numerous experiments were run to measure the relationships between physical objects and movement. Relationships were detected and turned into formulae, or laws. Mathematically, a corollary to Newton's second law of motion can be expressed by the following formula: $a = F/m$ where a = acceleration, F = force, and m = mass. This formula is a defined process model that describes the relationships between acceleration and mass when a force is applied. This defined model has been abstracted from many observations, and is now described as a law. Since the definition is repeatable, control is exercised through applying the definition faithfully. The noise in the relationships between acceleration, force, and mass is not intrusive and can usually be ignored. For most cases, this formula can be used to calculate acceptably accurate results for any of the variables.

For a systems development process description to be defined adequately to be used in a defined process control methodology, it would have to take into account at least the following:

A detailed, complete description of all inputs, including their content, precision, and media.

An equally detailed, complete description of all outputs.

A description of the processes necessary to complete the transformation from inputs to outputs, with reference to the specific tools and techniques used.

A detailed description of the skills, training, and capabilities of the people who would perform this transformation.

A description of what a "work hour" constitutes.

Let's consider what might be meant by the term "work hour." Is this an hour of work from a well-trained, well-educated, well-mentored, fully conscious, no personal problems, working in the morning after a cup of coffee engineer? Or is it an hour of work from someone else? The consistent application of the term "work hour" requires consistent productivity from each worker during every hour.

The control process for defined processes is the pert chart. For a pert chart to work, work hours must be consistently estimated and measured. Otherwise, every process has noise and the cumulative noise and inaccuracy sinks the whole project plan.

Discrepancies, incompleteness, and slippage accumulate as the project based on a network of interdependent, partially defined processes proceeds. As one task is completed and the results of the task are used to commence the next task, whatever noise occurred during the first task is carried on to the second task, which in turn generates its own noise. The first task is the "90% complete" project. 90% of the work estimated in the task is done, but only 30% of the product is done. The situation gets worse in the second task, and in other tasks down the line.

The process below could be from any commercial systems development methodology:

"*Optimize the Logical DataBase. Evaluate entity attributes, volume information, and security requirements to determine where record types should be split or combined. Prepare an entity to record/segment/table type cross-reference, distinguishing between existing databases which are to be shared and new databases which are to be created. When an entity is mapped to more than one record, include an attribute to field mapping.*"

I know from experience that, given the same inputs, no two people will produce the same outputs from this process. Even the same person won't generate the same outputs two times in a row. Why? The process definition is too loose, too vague. The vagueness is of necessity. If I watch and describe four thousand and seventeen people try to optimize a logical database, I will wind up with four thousand and seventeen different descriptions. The only way that I can abstract the descriptions into a model, or process description, like that above is to drop detail. Unfortunately, the detail that is dropped is the detail that is required for repeatability. The looseness and lack of detail in the above process abstraction is easily seen when I try to employ it to optimize my particular data model. The following areas (as a minimum) are too loosely defined for repeatability:

How do I evaluate the entity attributes?
What are the properties of the entity attributes?
Are the entity attributes part of a model? On what sort of tool?
How do I open the file?
What are the rules for splitting or combining?

How is a project supposed to be constructed from a methodology that relies on the defined process control model? A project manager starts a project by selecting and customizing the appropriate project template. The template consists of those processes appropriate for the type of work that is planned. He or she then estimates the work and assigns the tasks to team members. The resultant project plan shows all the work to be done, who is to do each piece of work, what the dependencies are, and the process instructions for converting the inputs to the outputs. Figure 5.3, Pert chart, shows a pert chart that is the product of such efforts.

Having a project plan like this gives the project manager a reassuring sense of being in control. He or she feels that they understand the work that is required to successfully complete the project. Everyone will do what the methodology and project plan says, and the project will be successfully completed. However, the task details on which the plan is based are incomplete because the underlying processes are complex and noisy. Because the definitions are incomplete, the dependencies are inaccurate. These estimates render the assignments and estimates useless.

A Pert chart is constructed using dependencies. When one or more tasks complete, dependent tasks can be started. The degree of noise in each systems development process makes it very hard to define "complete." The boundaries between the various assigned tasks start to become increasingly noisy until the project plan itself is chaotic. For a defined process to work, the noise that occurs each time a task is executed has to be within acceptable bounds; otherwise the operation of dependent processes is adversely affected. In a large network of dependent processes, the amount of noise rises exponentially as it is perpetrated throughout the network.

I single out pert charts as a significant problem. Pert charts are useful to think through and model a sequence of activities. They are disastrous when used to control a complex project. Pert chart-based project control

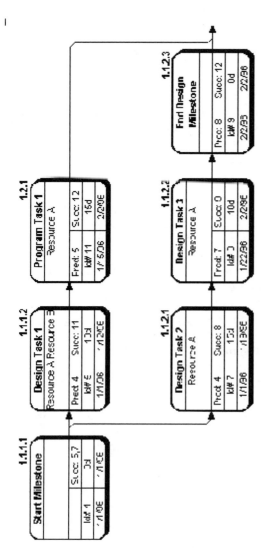

FIGURE 5.3: Pert chart

has led to systems development schizophrenia. Management thinks the pert chart models work in complex projects. It asks for progress reports based on the pert chart model. But the real work has very little to do with the pert chart. The work doesn't follow the pert chart. The work goes its own way, rapidly evolving after the first task to adapt to the complex problems at hand.

Developing complex software feels like running an obstacle course. Agility, flexibility and adaptability are required to succeed. Imagine a real obstacle course located at an Army training center. A team is asked to navigate the obstacle course as quickly as possible using a defined process. To prepare them, management has provided them with:

A map. The map isn't of this obstacle course, since no one has navigated it before. The map is of obstacle courses that others have run in the past.

A book containing descriptions of the various obstacles that have been found in other courses. Detailed instructions about how to approach, study, and navigate each obstacle course are provided.

A list of team assignments and expected progress. Management has painstakingly combined the map and book into what the team might find on this obstacle course. It has made team assignments. The assignments give team members specific duties at each obstacle. Each assignment tells them exactly what to do and allocates a fixed amount of time to complete it.

The team starts the obstacle course. Each member carries the map, the book, and the list of assignments. They study them as they go forward, doing exactly what the assignments say. The map is only a general and not an accurate description of the course, so reaching the first obstacle takes the team more time than was assigned. When it reaches the first obstacle, the obstacle only has vague similarities to the description in the book. Team members try to complete their individual assignments, but they are so inappropriate that several team members sustain injuries. The team has to devise an entirely new approach to get through the obstacle. Then each member has to fill out a time reporting form, including justification of why their the assignment took more time than expected to go over the obstacle!

Guilt entered the field of systems development when managers started using defined process control models to control and manage complex development projects. Managers lost control of the projects and were unable to predict the results of projects. The heavyweight methodologies provided management with plans that included time and cost estimates. The project manager used these estimates to contract functionality, time, quality, and costs with the customer. When the customer found that something they expected was not included, that quality was low, that dates slipped, they were furious. They had trusted the project manager's plans and estimates, but the project manager didn't deliver.

The project manager's management licensed the heavyweight methodology from a reputable vendor. The vendor told the project manager to follow the instructions in the methodology to plan and get reliable, predictable results. The methodology was well known, so it must work! But it didn't work!! The manager thinks,

"I did what the methodology told me to do. The developers must not have done what the methodology told them to do. Maybe they didn't report their progress accurately. Maybe they didn't follow the methodology's directions. They had failed to successfully complete well-described processes that a methodology vendor had told me would lead to predictable results. Those developers are to blame!!"

Guilt arose, and with guilt came apathy. Workers who do their best, but consistently fail to live up to their own expectations, eventually stop trying to do their best. It never seems to be good enough or appreciated.

The traditional, defined software development process is broken. Assuming that most projects have a high degree of predictability, it doesn't adequately detect the noise within complex projects or facilitate empirical responses to assess and correctly respond to the noise. Since the noise is unnoticed and ignored, the results are unpredictable. This incorrect formulation has led to innumerable cancelled projects, many wasted efforts to "get it right", and an overall failure to successfully manage software development. More significantly, many marketplace opportunities have been missed and vast sums of capital have been wasted. Unnecessary human suffering and stress have been borne.

5.4 Why Scrum Works

I said earlier that Scrum was simple and straightforward. There are no complicated process descriptions and there are no abstractions. Scrum starts with the tenet that very few activities in system development projects are identical and will generate identical output. Scrum expects every process to be unexpected.

When activities are so complicated and complex that they can't be defined in advance and aren't repeatable, they require the **empirical** process control model. Scrum employs the empirical process control model. Scrum regularly inspects activities to see what is occurring and empirically adapts activities to produce desired and predictable outcomes.

Chemical companies have advanced polymer plants that require empirical controls. Some chemical processes haven't been defined well enough for the plant to operate safely and repeatably using a defined process control model. Noise has rendered statistical controls ineffective. Frequent inspections and verification are required to successfully produce a batch. As chemical processes become better understood and the technology improves, the plants become more automated. However, assuming predictability too soon is the recipe for an industrial catastrophe.

The heart of Scrum is assessing the condition of activities and empirically determining what to do next. This determination arises from the experience, training, and common sense. Once a process is started, it is frequently inspected, assessed, and adjusted. The people inspecting the process expect the unexpected, monitor for it, and adapt as needed.

Empirical process control models are elegantly simple. They employ feedback mechanisms to monitor and adapt to the unexpected, providing regularity and predictability. The actors in a Scrum team empirically devise and execute the best processes possible based on their skills, experience, and the situation in which they find themselves. Figure 5.4, Empirical Management Model, depicts the empirical process control feedback loop used by Scrum.

"I" is input, or the requirements, technology - the team that will build a product increment from the requirements and technology.

"Process" is a thirty day iteration called a Sprint.

"C" is the control unit that monitors Scrum progress at Daily Scrum meetings and at the end of each Sprint.

"O" is the incremental product built during each iteration. [Peitgen][1]

During a Sprint, a team empirically determines how to build a product increment (Output) given the requirements and the technology available to them (Input). The team draws on its collective skills to accomplish its common goals. Teammates advise and assist each other, and together the team hunts down whatever resources it might need. The team is left alone to self-organize and forge a product from the requirements and the technology that it has been given.

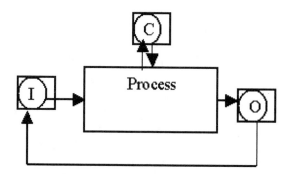

FIGURE 5.4: Empirical Management Model

---

[1]New development projects build the first increment from scratch.

The Scrum process controls complex activities. Ongoing inspections provide the information necessary to empirically determine what to do next. Control, or "C", is implemented through daily status meetings, Daily Scrums. During the Daily Scrums, management and the team inspect and measure the process to see if the progress and results are acceptable. If they are in fact acceptable, nothing happens until the next inspection. If they are not acceptable, there is still time to restore the process to acceptable performance levels.

At the end of each Sprint, there is another control. This control is called the Sprint Review. Sprint output is inspected. What the team has actually built is evaluated. Management, customers and the team inspect the product, reviewing an actual demonstration of working, executable product increment. People have less trouble making decisions when they can see their options right in front of them, so the product is demonstrated on a computer. Management, customers, and the team then decide what to do next; they adapt to what they have seen. The team may be given more training, the team may be recomposed, or more tools may be brought in. Anything that affects the ability of the team to build the next product increment can be changed.

Some of my customers have assigned process engineers to Scrum projects. They wanted to leverage the project experience by recording, abstracting, and formalizing the work. They intended to revert to the defined process control model and pert charts once they figured out what Scrum was about. The process engineers watched, interviewed, and recorded the work. When they went to add the work definitions to the organization's methodology, each project had to become a new, unique template. Every new project either addressed a new business domain or utilized a new set of technology. These customers concluded that the activities recorded were so complex that they couldn't be defined or abstracted. Each project was unique. Scrum is a harness on complex processes, a constraint on complexity.

As an alternative, these customers turned to knowledge management solutions to build a repository of organizational experience about building systems. They put the processes from their licensed defined methodologies in the knowledge base. They added their unique processes for version control, builds, testing, password management, requisitioning material, and other processes used to run a systems development project. The knowledge repository became the institutional expert, used when the team needed to know how to do something. The knowledge repository was not used to plan and drive work; instead, it was used as a reference for how to do work. The knowledge repository evolved as new knowledge was captured and new technologies were brought in.

There is nothing wrong with such abstracted process knowledge as long as it is recognized as incomplete and only appropriate for guidance. It cannot be expected to produce repeatability. Patterns represent just such knowledge, providing a framework within which to address problems [ScrumPattern]. Solid engineering teams draw on patterns, techniques, and specific technology knowledge to solve problems. Scrum teaches teams to rely on their wits, training, teammates, and fellow engineers.

5.5   Case Studies

In the following examples, the empirical process control model was implemented because the underlying activity could not be defined adequately enough to be repeatable. The underlying activity was complex.

The first example shows what happens when I think I can pick my daughter up from college without checking things out. She calls me on her cell phone when she's ready and tells me where to come. The process flow used to be: (1) receive call for a ride, (2) drive to location, and (3) pick up daughter. The reception on her cell phone isn't always great. There have been times when I thought that I heard her say to pick her up at her dorm, but she really said to pick her up someplace else. As a result of the noise in this communication, I drive to the wrong place. I've put in empirical controls to try to reduce the noise. This process is now: (1) receive call for a ride, (2) try to get her to repeat location if noise occurs, (3) ask wife and other daughter if this sounds like the right place to go, (4) drive there, (5) wait for a short time to see if she shows up, (6) if she doesn't show up, call home to see if she's called, (7) go to where she really is, and (8) pick her up. Since the process is noisy, I've had to add frequent monitoring and empirically adapt to the observations. Because the cell phone technology is uncertain and the location requirements change unpredictably, employing the empirical model gives me the level of inspection and control that ensures I arrive at the right place most of the time.

The second example happened when Scrum was implemented at Individual, Inc., in order to help the company develop another product, Corporate NewsPage (CNP). Individual, Inc. published customized news at customer sites through CNP. The product development team was under pressure to turn out a new release, but the team was busy porting the prior release from the base Sun platform to HP and IBM platforms. Both HP and IBM had released new operating systems, and the team had been caught unprepared. The technology they were using had changed, and the complexity of their project had skyrocketed. Suddenly they had to change operating systems, in addition to developing additional functionality for the new release.

Because the team was using Scrum, an empirical process, it stopped and reevaluated their priorities. Rather than doing as it had always done, the team asked whether its ordinary practices made sense under these circumstances. A little investigation showed that sales had not yet sold any sites that would use the IBM port, and had sold only one HP installation. By taking a step back from its work and evaluating the situation, the team was able to skip the ports and move on to tackle the new release. Was this just a case of using common sense? Yes, but that is the core of empirical processes.

C H A P T E R   6

Why Does Scrum Work?

Software development is an activity that creates new products. Therefore it is more akin to new product development than to the manufacturing models that it has been forced to fit in the last 20 years. This new world-view represents a Kuhnian paradigm shift for software development because new product development processes require a new set of practices rooted in self-organization and knowledge creation to cope with the inherent activities of research and creativity involved in creating something new. —

6.1   Understanding Scrum

A few years ago, I started a project at a telecom company. During the first week I explained Scrum. After the brief, one-hour explanation that described the basic Scrum practices one of the members of the team asked me:

"If all we are doing in a Scrum meeting is to report what we did within the last day, report new issues, and state what we are going to be doing in the next day, why don't we write a database program on the web that captures this information. That way we won't miss any time at the Scrum meetings."

It seemed to others like a reasonable request. If these Scrum meetings were only capturing this information, why should we meet every day at the same time and talk? People could write their own statuses at any time. They could see what other people were doing if they wanted. Leave issues for management to resolve.

It was tempting to replace the meetings with the software; however, some things, like human interactions, should not be automated, so my answer to that request was:

"Scrum meetings do much more for a team than just capturing information. They don't only make everyone capture what they did, but it makes everyone say it in front of everybody else. That way everyone listens to what others are doing and they can offer to help them later. They don't only make everyone say what the issues are, but it makes everyone say it face to face to their management. This forces everyone to have courage and to be honest, and gives everyone a tool to put pressure on management about resolving issues. It also makes everyone promise in front of everyone else what you will be working on next, so it puts everyone's credibility and trust to the test. Scrum is about deep social interactions that build trust among team members."

Clearly, I knew something they didn't and it made a difference in the decision of changing or not changing Scrum. This is precisely the difference between knowing how to apply Scrum and knowing why it works. In most cases it is sufficient to know how it works, but knowing *why* it works is especially helpful when one proposes to either change some of the Scrum practices, or to incorporate other practices like XP practices.

I have found that the following related views are very useful to understand why Scrum works:

The new product development view of Scrum

The risk management and predictability view of Scrum

The Kuhnian view of Scrum

Knowledge Creation view of Scrum

The Complexity Science view of Scrum

Anthropological view of Scrum

The System Dynamics view of Scrum

The Psychological view of Scrum

The Football metaphor

These views are important to realize that while Scrum practices may look simple and unsophisticated on the surface, the dynamics they control and create have profound implications. My intent is not to provide a comprehensive and exhaustive explanation of the concepts involved – that would take several volumes with thousands of references. Instead, I want to provide a simple explanation of these concepts so that, you, the reader of this book, can build useful mental models of Scrum.

These views are related and they build the argument for this book: software development is like new product development not like manufacturing. This difference is revolutionary, and it leads to a completely new way of thinking about what software is and how to build it.

6.2 The New Product Development View of Scrum

Traditional software development methods are in a crisis because they cannot control software development despite their elaborate process models. But this crisis can be explained in terms of the incorrect assumptions that are made about software and software development by traditional methods.

First and foremost, the assumption that software is manufactured and that it therefore should follow similar processes to manufacturing is incorrect.

Manufacturing is about assembling the same model of something such as a radio, an automobile, or a plane over and over again. But software is about creating something new because - even if reusable parts are used - the configuration or arrangement of them will be new. For example, consider what happens when one uses a library or a component in an application. The component is parameterized and more often than not, some of its functionality is overridden.

This is a fundamental assumption that has haunted the software industry for the last 20 years or so, ever since Watts Humphrey prodded us to use a manufacturing model in software through the CMM (The capability maturity model). Humphrey borrowed the maturity model from MMM (Manufacturing maturity model) that Crosby exposed in his landmark book "Quality is Free"[Crosby], and that has left us with a history or 20 years of software development that has tried to emulate manufacturing process models.

In manufacturing, it makes perfect sense to demand "repeatable and defined" processes that assemble an identical model in an assembly line. But software has different demands: it is different for every arrangement.

Therefore, software development better fits the model of new product development. But creating something new requires research, creativity and learning. These activities are based on different assumptions and require a completely different way to estimate, plan, track, and manage than those techniques used in the manufacturing of products.

For starters, research and creativity activities are much less predictable. They may have bounds, like creating a design of a new VCR model, but they have many more options than manufacturing an instance of a given model.

Because software requirements for an application are never specified identically or even completely, software development always involves research. And because every application is different, their designs, by necessity, are always new. They can be similar and use patterns like MVC (model-view-controller), PAC (presentation-abstraction-control), or a Pipes and Filters architecture, but when they get down to a specific implementation, the business objects, the business rules, and the transactions and services required are different.

Nonaka and Takeuchi, in their famous Harvard Business Review article [Takeuchi and Nonaka], show how innovative companies create new products. In their analysis of ten of the most competitive and innovative companies on the planet they found that they require:

Built-in instability. Team members are given the freedom to do research and creativity but at the same time they are expected to produce up-to high standards.

Self-organizing project teams. A project team takes on a self-organizing character as it is driven to a state of zero information, where prior knowledge does not apply. Ambiguity and fluctuation abound in this state. Left to stew, the process begins to create its own dynamic order and the team starts to create its own agenda, taking risks, and creating new concepts.

Overlapping development phases. In an environment where some of the requirements are discovered while simultaneously something is created with the information at hand, it is imperative that the phases of discovery, invention, and testing overlap to drive the creation of a new product to completion through self-consistency. Most problems in new product development arise when the phases of the project are separated. Empirically, this overlap in phases enhances shared responsibility and cooperation, stimulates involvement and commitment, sharpens a problem-solving focus, encourages initiative taking, develops diversified skills, and heightens sensitivity toward market conditions.

Multi-learning. Teams must stay in close touch with outside sources of information so that they can respond quickly to changes in the environment. This learning manifests itself along two dimensions: 1) Across multiple levels (individual, group, and organizations), and 2) across multiple functions.

Subtle control. Although teams are largely on their own because they need this freedom to be creative and effective, management must establish some controls to prevent instability, ambiguity and tension from turning into uncontrolled chaos. These controls are:

Selecting team members and constantly balancing the team.

Creating an open work environment.

Encouraging constant communication with the customer.

Establishing an evaluation and reward system based on group performance.

Managing the differences in rhythm throughout the development phases.

Tolerating and anticipating mistakes.

Encouraging dependent teams to also become self-organizing.

Transfer of learning. Seeding new teams with team members of previous teams.

All of these are fundamentals of new product development; since Scrum adopts this paradigm, they are also fundamental to the correct implementation of Scrum.

6.3   The Risk Management and Predictability View of Scrum

> **Scrum advocates a new paradigm for software development that requires self-organization, while simultaneously providing risk-reducing practices to tame this new kind of organization.**
> —

Another useful way to look at Scrum is as a *risk reduction system*. This is a particularly useful way to look at Scrum, especially from the management perspective. In my experience risk and uncertainty have always been there in software development, but the advantage of Scrum is its ability to recognize them and to provide practices to tame them. Where do risk and uncertainty come from in software development?

The section above outlines a new way of doing software development that is based on the assumption that software is more like new product development. This assumption implies that there is a great deal of research and creativity that requires self-organization, learning, and overlapping development phases. However, the nature of these activities is arguably less predictable and involves more risk and uncertainty. As a consequence, Scrum provides new ways of estimating, planning, tracking and managing that cut through these risks and uncertainties.

Risk of not pleasing the customer. Scrum copes with the risk of not pleasing the customer by allowing the customer to see the product on a constant basis. Whenever possible, Scrum prefers to have a customer on-site but it mandates that the customer sees working software at least every Sprint. This validates the efforts of the team in providing the functionality promised at the Sprint Review Meeting and reprioritizing other functionality to be worked on at the Sprint Planning Meeting.

Risk of not completing all functionality. Scrum copes with the risk of not delivering all the functionality in a release by developing functionality in a prioritized way through Sprints. This ensures that all the high priority functionality will be delivered and that only lower priority functionality is missed.

Risk of poor estimating and planning. Scrum manages this risk through the Daily Scrums by always providing small estimates that are tracked within a Daily Scrum cycle, and through the Sprint cycle that has an invariant set of Product Backlog assigned to it. Within a Daily Scrum cycle, Scrum tolerates the risk that activities within this window may not be completed, but it provides management control to avoid errors greater than this cycle. Within the Sprint cycle, Scrum tolerates the fact that not all goals of the Sprint may be completed, but it adjusts its goals through the Sprint Review and the Sprint Planning Meeting.

Risk of not resolving issues promptly. Scrum puts the burden of proof on management by requiring daily active management. In Scrum, the role of management is bi-directional, in that management also reports to the staff how it is resolving issues through the Daily Scrums.

Risk of not being able to complete the development cycle. Scrum ensures that there aren't any major problems with the development cycle by delivering working software every Sprint. If there are any issues with engineering practices such as configuration management, regression testing, system testing or release management, Scrum irons out all the details by forcing a working release. In some cases, these issues actually impede the complete delivery of a Sprint, but the advantage is that the team is forced to confront the issues and solve them.

Risk of taking too much work and changing expectations. Scrum prevents the risk of changing the expectations of the customer and the team by disallowing any changes to the Product Backlog associated with a Sprint. That way the team feels that their goal is respected and the customer has clear expectations.

6.4   The Kuhnian View of Scrum

> Scrum represents a paradigm shift in software development. Scrum breaks the tradition of old paradigms and metaphors because it is based on the paradigm, practices and metaphors of new product development; therefore, it provides practices that support research, creativity, learning and knowledge creation; activities that in turn require a self-organizing structure.   —

Thomas Kuhn, one of the great philosophers of science, argues that scientific, and therefore technological revolutions come in cycles of "regular science", "crises" and "revolutionary paradigm shifts"[Kuhn]. His argument is based on the piecemeal refinement and higher demands for accuracy that each new theory brings.

At first, a theory better explains an event in the world, but then, as more details are calculated with it, it breaks because it can't account for some events or predicts results that are different from observed values. Eventually, as more and more "defects" are found with an existing theory, these defects give rise to a crisis that is only resolved by a new theory that better explains and accounts for the observed phenomena. Software development does not escape this historical evolution.

Software development saw a paradigm shift in the late 80s, when it was assumed that software behaved and could be controlled like a manufacturing product. This brought many good things. For example, all the tasks that took place in software development were defined, as exemplified by the CMM's KPAs (key process areas).

However, this paradigm has also put software development in a crisis. It is nearly impossible to develop software in short periods of time, with high quality and with a low budget using the "defined and repeatable" process approach. And as I have explained in the section above "The new product development view of Scrum", Scrum makes a radically different assumption about software development. This underlying assumption is so different that it is our estimation and hope that it will trigger a paradigm shift.

As of now, Scrum represents a competing worldview when compared to the many other styles of software development or business organization, but one that, given its success and simplicity, will convince the world of its superiority in the long term.

6.5   Knowledge Creation View of Scrum

I have proposed above that software development is the result of creating new products, and that by necessity it requires research and creativity. However, the commonality among research and creativity is knowledge creation.

The fact that we gather requirements for an application strongly indicates that they are in tacit form, and as we make design decisions we acquire knowledge that we eventually capture in the code or in an executable model. From this perspective, software is nothing else than *codified and explicit knowledge.*

Explicit knowledge means knowledge transmittable in a systematic language. For example, in software development, code, and documents, UML (Unified Modeling Language) models and graphics are explicit knowledge. Explicit knowledge is in sharp contrast with *tacit knowledge,* which is based on experience and typically reflected in our intuitions and reactions but not externalized. In software development we often find people with special abilities and knowledge that is not externalized. Good examples of this are software users, domain experts, and experienced programmers.

From the perspective of knowledge creation, Scrum has the effect of promoting the creation of knowledge [Takeuchi and Nonaka] through cycles of socialization, externalization, combination, and internalization of knowledge. See Figure 6.1, Knowledge conversion.

Socialization is direct conveyance of tacit knowledge through shared experience.

Externalization is the process of articulating tacit knowledge into explicit concepts.

Combination is a process of systematizing concepts into a knowledge system.

Internalization means embodying explicit knowledge in tacit, operational knowledge.

The daily Scrum meetings are a good example of this cycle. First, the tacit knowledge of a team member is socialized at a Scrum meeting. The externalization of this knowledge typically results in items in the Sprint Backlog, but it can be simply useful knowledge for other team members. Other team members can then combine this knowledge with more externalized or tacit knowledge and once again internalize it to make use of it during a day of work. The continuous application of this cycle through the Scrum practices throughout the organization results in the Knowledge

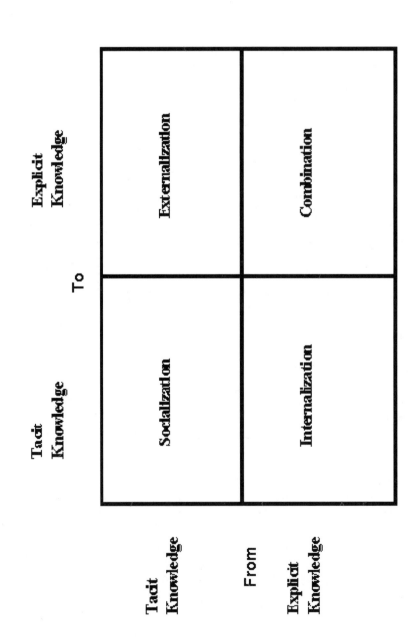

FIGURE 6.1: Knowledge Conversion. (From: Nonaka I., Takeuchi H., *The Knowledge Creating Company*, Oxford University Press, Oxford 1995.)

Spiral that spreads knowledge rapidly throughout the organization. See Figure 6.2, Knowledge spiral.

A Scrum team creates knowledge through these mechanisms:

Sharing tacit knowledge. Example: Developers exchanging ideas about requirements or design in a Scrum meeting or while working in pairs or triads with other developers.

Creating concepts. Example: The creation of design models like packages, classes, relationships and interactions.

Justifying concepts. Example: Developers validating requirements and designs.

Building an archetype. Example: Building a prototype.

Cross leveling of knowledge. Basically this starts the cycle all over again.

Though they are listed here sequentially, it should be clear that a developer is free to move between them adaptively.

6.6   The Complexity Science View of Scrum

I have proposed in the above sections that because Scrum assumes that software must be a new product requiring research and creativity, its organization must consist of self-organizing project teams and must have overlapping development phases. That means that the Scrum organization or processes cannot be statically defined or for that matter repeated. You can only hope to repeat the application of the Scrum practices but they will lead to different organizational or process arrangements every time.

However, to really understand the dynamics of self-organization, we must delve into Complexity Science.

6.6.1   Definitions

Complexity Science is the name commonly used to describe a set of interdisciplinary studies that describe self-organizing systems (SOS). These systems are so pervasive and are found in almost every science: Physics, Chemistry, Biology, Sociology, Political Science, and Anthropology. For example, an ant colony, the brain, the immune system, a Scrum team, and New York City are self-organizing systems. It is important to notice, however, that:

All human organization is self-organization.

Even in the case where some agents, like in military organizations, dictate the organization of some other agents, eventually the subordinate agents organize themselves into the mandated organization. Clearly, this kind-of self-organization is very inflexible. Compare that to the self-organization of a SWAT team. It still operates within some rules and bounds but their self-organization is much more flexible.

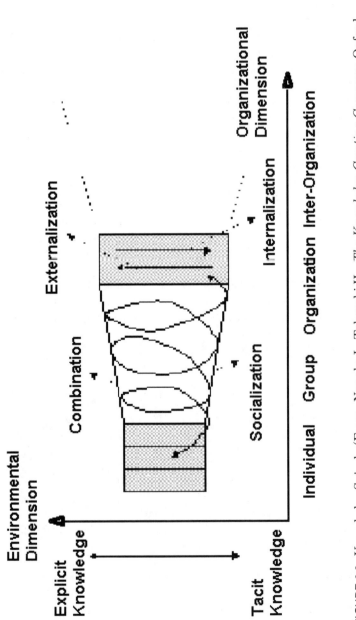

FIGURE 6.2: Knowledge Spiral. (From: Nonaka I., Takeuchi H., *The Knowledge Creating Company*, Oxford University Press, Oxford 1995.)

It is said that an organization is more *ordered* as the organization is better defined. For example, an assembly line in a factory is very well defined. It is said that an organization is more *chaotic* if it has a more dynamic configuration with less static patterns, for example, toddlers running around in a large room. It is said that an organization is at the edge of chaos if the organization lives in a state where there is order in chaos. Examples of this type of organization are SWAT teams, basketball teams, soccer teams and Scrum teams.

6.6.2   Features

Self-organizing systems share many features and Scrum has good examples of each of them [Holland98][Holland95]:

They are composed of **Agents**. Agents are independent actors that can act autonomously. For example, developers, the Scrum Master, and the Product Owner are agents.

They are **Open Systems**. They exchange energy, mass or information with their surroundings. For example, a Scrum team exchanges information with a customer and with other teams like the testing and production environment support teams.

They are **Dynamic**. Their state is constant flux. A Scrum team is constantly reorganizing on different time-scales: minute-by-minute on daily activities, daily at the Scrum meetings, and monthly at the Sprint planning meetings.

Flows. Flows mean exchange of mass, energy or information among agents. For example, in Scrum teams, there is constant information flow 1) among the developers during a typical development day, 2) among the developers and the Scrum Master at the Scrum meetings, and 3) between the customer and the Scrum team at planning meetings and on a daily basis.

They rely on **Dense Local Interactions.** The agents interact with each other according to rules and exchange information through flows *constantly and periodically.* For example, Scrum team members are constantly sharing information and knowledge through the day, and periodically at Scrum meetings, End of Sprint demonstrations and Sprint Planning meetings.

Emergence. Emergence is another way of saying that the whole is greater than the sum of the parts. Rules that are almost absurdly simple can generate coherent, emergent phenomena. For example, the rule about not changing the assignment of product backlog to a Sprint has deep repercussions. The customer can still add features but the Scrum team is undisturbed because its goal is respected, so its credibility is easier to maintain, as a result there is more trust from the client in the team. Therefore, this rule results in the emergence of a more stable customer-team relationship.

Building Blocks and Aggregation. Sometimes also called multi-scale effects. Building blocks are recurrent structures that are used as the parts of a Lego set. Aggregation is the ability to combine these building blocks. At each level of scale there are different building blocks that aggregate to form the building blocks of the next level of scale. Aggregations are typically based on recurring interactions that depend on pre-established flows. For example, a business organization can be seen as a collection of process teams and support teams. One of these support teams is the IT organization, which in turn is composed of application development teams, production environment support teams, testing teams, etc. The application development teams can in turn be made of one or more Scrum teams, which in turn are composed of individual developers.

Tagging. Tags are temporary labels on agents or artifacts that can be used for signaling and facilitating the creation of aggregates. For example, in a Scrum meeting, people are temporarily tagged as chickens and pigs. By definition people only involved in the development of the system like managers are chickens, and people committed to delivering the system, such as developers, are pigs. Another example of tagging is when a developer is tagged as an apprentice or a mentor (sometimes also called a coach or an architect).

Diversity and Specialization. Diversity states that there are many kinds of agents in a self-organizing system. Specialization in most cases is the root case of diversity. For example in a Scrum team, there are Product Owners, Scrum Masters and developers. Among developers there is also specialization and diversity. For example, a developer may specialize in: databases, Java, configuration management, requirements gathering, unit testing, etc.

Internal and Shared Models. Each agent in the system typically has its own internal models. In most cases, self-organizing systems also have shared models among some agents in the system. The internal models are typically affected by the flows during interactions among agents. For example, in a Scrum team, the Sprint Goal, the current Backlog, the requirements, and the architecture are shared models, with each of the developers having their own internal models.

Nonlinear Dynamics. Sometimes also dubbed non-linearity. Non-linear Dynamics means that the feedback loops in an agent colony obey non-linear rules. This is a characteristic of positive or negative feedback loops. For example, the combined effects of developers sharing knowledge among themselves, trusting each other, communicating often with a customer, and learning more about the technology they are working with have non-linear effects in their productivity over time. A team may double their productivity in their first 3 months working together. But it may double it again in the fourth month alone. In the best cases, this productivity can increase ten-fold (1000%) after a few months of working in a Scrum team.

6.6.3   Scrum Organization, Processes and Roles

A self-organizing system relies on the above features to function. However, one key characteristic of a self-organizing system is to be able to adapt. Because of this characteristic, self-organizing systems are similar to live systems. In fact, all living systems are self-organizing systems but not all self-organizing systems are live systems.

In that sense, a software development team is described as being more agile or more "alive" as its ability to adapt increases. Scrum rates very high in adaptability. Why? Throughout this book we have learned that Scrum doesn't use very many hierarchical controls of management, processes or even role definitions. The **organization** pecking order inside a Scrum team is really based on knowledge relationships: whoever knows more about a subject takes a higher pecking order in a discussion. The **development tasks** are reorganized dynamically, minute-by-minute in developers' collaborations, day-by-day in Scrum meetings, and Sprint-by-Sprint in Sprint planning meetings, so there aren't any static process definitions. Instead tasks, like organizations, are arranged dynamically using short feedback cycles. Finally, the **roles** of developers on a Scrum team also adapt in short time cycles. Where more traditional organizations call for the definition of static roles, Scrum developers can change hats dynamically, often passing as analysts, testers, coders, designers, architects and integrators in a single day. Simply said, everyone does everything that is in his or her power to deliver the system.

This type of organization doesn't fall into any traditional organizational structure or process structure. Instead, Scrum has a self-organizing structure close to edge of chaos. The dynamic structures are typically pairs or triads of developers that are working on a piece of the system. These pairs are formed for many different reasons: 1) mentor/apprentice relationships, 2) cross-functional relationships like domain expert/analyst/ developer teams, and 3) expert/expert team to achieve high levels of creativity and productivity. Scrum teams are therefore very dynamic and can be better understood as people (the adaptive agents) capable of dynamic behavior who develop software through dense local people-to-people and people-to-software interactions.

The extremely high ability to constantly reconfigure or adapt is driven in Scrum teams by the basic Scrum practices:

First and foremost, the **Scrum team values** allow diverse team members to share information, trust each other, collaborate in tasks, and truly commit to deliver the system. The Scrum team values define the interactions among team members and ensure that there are constant flows of information among them. These flows in turn build the shared models of the team. These values ensure that mentor/apprentice and cross-functional collaborations and interactions are successful.

Daily Scrum meetings. Each and every day, the team reflects where it is, what issues it has and where it is going, and adapts accordingly. Scrum meetings ensure that everyone knows what everyone else is doing, promoting opportunities for mentoring or collaboration.

Demo after Sprint. The Demo after the Sprint allows the team to give feedback to the customer on what the team accomplished, and for the customer to give feedback to the team. This allows the team to adapt according to the customer feedback and for the customer to adapt according to the work presented.

End of Sprint and **Sprint Planning** meetings. Every Sprint the team reflects on what it has accomplished at the Sprint in the End of Sprint meeting, and reconfigures in the Sprint Planning meeting to develop new functionality.

Adaptation and Natural Selection

It is interesting to see what researchers in Complexity Science say about organizations that live close to the edge of chaos [Kauffman93]:

There is an optimum of adaptability in systems that self-organize right at the edge of chaos.

Natural selection chooses configurations that are more apt to adapt.

Coevolving systems (ecosystems) whose members have tuned their structures to live close to the edge of chaos live longer.

Since Scrum teams live closer to the edge of chaos this means that:

Scrum teams are more adaptable than traditional teams that organize with defined organizations, defined processes and defined roles.

Scrum teams are able to survive longer i.e. stay in stable configurations for longer periods of time, because adaptability *selects* them to live longer.

Scrum teams coevolve better and longer with other teams that have similar structures. For example, if - in addition to the application development teams - the business organization uses Scrum and other adaptive techniques to organize itself, the whole eco-system will coevolve and live longer. This explains why Scrum works so well with business organizations that use adaptive methods, and with software teams that use agile methods like XP.

Scrum practices, though simple, indeed have deep implications for agility and adaptability.

6.7   Anthropological View of Scrum

The agents discussed above are humans, and therefore their interactions are best understood in the context of Anthropology[Harris97]. Basically, practicing Scrum changes the culture of an organization because Scrum comes with new values, beliefs, language, rules, roles, and practices. And some Scrum practices can also be seen as ceremonies and rites, like the Scrum meetings or the Sprint planning meetings.

For example, there is an immense culture building value in holding the Scrum meetings at the same place at the same time because this *ceremony* has the effect of bonding and jelling a group of individuals. Other examples are having the rule of "pigs and chickens", going around the room and taking the same places in the room every day, and collecting one dollar from people who are late.

However, changing cultures is one of the most difficult changes one can ever make. Here are some best practices that allow us to do it more effectively:

Support. Get the support from upper management. This will allow you to report success and correlate it to Scrum at the end of projects, and will allow Scrum to spread throughout the organization. This support is also important at the Sprint Planning Meetings, where the customer is heavily involved.

Language. Cultures create languages and languages create cultures, so introduce the Scrum vocabulary and enforce it.

Roles and Mentors. Seed your organization with mentors that already know the Scrum process. They typically are Scrum Masters but in some cases they can also be developers.

Values. Reinforce the Scrum values. For example, by providing weekly "brown bag" lunches where different topics are explored: patterns, refactoring, new technologies, etc.; you can reinforce the "sharing knowledge" value. Another example is keeping and publishing an honest Sprint Backlog, that promotes courage, honesty, and trust. Another example is introducing people that are in the habit of being "focused and committed" that can serve as role models.

Beliefs. Explain Scrum to the team members by holding presentations and publishing documents that show why Scrum is different.

Practices and Rules. Practice the Scrum practices and enforce all of its rules. Remember, every rule has a good reason to exist, and it results in emergent behavior.

6.8   The System Dynamics View of Scrum

In the section above where I discussed the Complexity Science view of Scrum, I said that flows and dense local interactions were needed among the developers of a software project. However, I said nothing about the efficiency of such flows and interactions. In this section I will expose some of the Scrum flow efficiency through the perspective of System Dynamics.

System Dynamics is the study of organizations by means of feedback loops. A little bit of history is in order. In the early 1980's there was a great interest in making business processes more efficient, in particular those that were concerned with managing inventories. Inventories cost money, so having "idle" money sitting somewhere is never a good idea. On the other hand, not having enough raw materials at any given time can effectively stop a production line. So having *minimal but sufficient* inventories is ideal.

To understand the conceptual solution above is not all that hard; however, to come up with practical solutions that actually implement this conceptual solution is much harder. Eventually luminaries like Eli Goldratt [Goldratt], figured out that smaller inventories could be maintained by using short feedback loops that moved smaller quantities into the inventory. Identical solutions came from MIT's Sloan business school as the solution of the famous "beer game": move smaller amounts in shorter periods of time.

But how does "inventory management" relate to software development? Well, any resource can be seen the same way including "developer's time", because whether companies use it appropriately or not, they have to pay either salaries or consulting fees. The virtues of Scrum from this perspective, are that Scrum provides very many feedback cycles at different levels of scale:

Measuring all resource inventory levels constantly and changing fast in small amounts how developers use their time.

Simply said, Scrum is the solution of the beer game applied to software development because Scrum makes it impossible for developer's time to go to waste or for issues to impede development. Here developer's time can be seen as "inventory" and issues impeding development can be seen as lack of inventory of another resource. For example, if a testing environment is not available, this can be seen as not having enough "testing environment inventory."

Software as well as business organization have been seen in this light before. For example, Jerry Weinberg, one of the greatest software gurus, bases most of his analysis in system dynamics archetypes [Weinberg]. Peter Senge, from MIT's Sloan school has also developed notation and techniques to document people interactions through system dynamics techniques [Senge].

6.9   The Psychological View of Scrum

I have said much about people interactions, but I haven't explained what happens to people working in a Scrum team from the inside out. Scrum has different effects on people. For most, belonging to a Scrum team gets them to be highly focused, effective, cooperative and committed over time. However, there are also the scant few that don't like Scrum, and that's because Scrum always tells the truth about everyone.

However, for the majority that do benefit from Scrum, their state of consciousness can be better explained by the concept of "flow". Mihaly Csikszentmihalyi from the University of Chicago defines "flow" as the state of an individual having the following characteristics:

They are working to accomplish clear goals. Both the Scrum Planning meetings, and the Daily Scrum meetings help define clear goals.

They get immediate feedback about their progress toward these goals. The daily Scrum meetings give this feedback.

They must use significant skill to achieve their goals. Scrum requires a balance of individuals with at least 50% of them to be experts, but Scrum also promotes fast learning, so skills transfer rapidly and effectively among the team members.

They are in control of the work and have it in their power to accomplish it. Scrum assigns work from the Product Backlog and creates a Sprint Backlog that controls the work at all times. Also, Scrum allows the elevation and resolution of issues through the daily Scrum meetings, removing any impediments from the way of the developers.

They can concentrate on the goals without being distracted. Scrum provides a comfort shell for developers where the Scrum Master acts as a firewall.

They become deeply involved in the work. Scrum drives individuals to focus, commit and excel.

They focus on the work and lose concern for themselves.

They experience an altered sense of time.

They consistently produce at high levels of accomplishment.

Scrum allows developers to concentrate most of their time in developing software, and by doing so developers enter "flow" state.

6.10   The Football Metaphor

This is a somewhat unrelated view of Scrum compared to the ones above and it is only provided here to explain Scrum's name. The first thing that people ask about Scrum is about the meaning of the word Scrum itself. Some think that it is an acronym; some think that it is an obscure word, but as said earlier in this book, Scrum comes from Rugby, and is a dense circle of people that typically is split by members of the Rugby teams that fight for possession of the ball:

One of the charms of Rugby Union game is the infinite variety of its possible tactics. Whatever tactics a team aims to adopt, the first essential is a strong and skillful pack of forwards capable of winning initial possession from the set pieces. For with the ball in its hands, a team is in a position to dictate tactics, which will make the best use of its own particular talents, at the same time probing for and exposing weaknesses in the opposing team. The ideal team has fast and clever half-backs and three-quarters who, with running, passing, and shrewd kicking, will make sure that the possession won by the forwards is employed to the maximum embarrassment of the opposing team.

The external perception of a Scrum meeting might look closer to a Scrum in Rugby, but from an information perspective, a Scrum meeting is closer to a football huddle: it is a short meeting to plan the next down. As such, we can draw the analogies in Table 1, Football metaphor.

Scrum Practice	Football Practice
Scrum meetings	Huddle
A day of work	a down
First and ten	a Sprint
Scoring (Touch down, field goal)	Delivery to production

TABLE 6.1: Football metaphor

Of course, this is just a metaphor, and all metaphors eventually break down, but it matches fairly close if we leave the analysis at the above level of abstraction.

CHAPTER 7

Advanced Scrum Applications

> Scrum works for all projects - projects of all sizes, projects that involve multiple applications reusing components; projects where extremely high quality is expected, and business projects. —

7.1 Applying Scrum to Multiple Related Projects

In the previous chapters Scrum has been described in one-project applications. However, in large companies, many interrelated projects typically are developed at the same time with resources shared among these projects.

In these cases, the complexity of the environment is magnified by at least one level of magnitude, and it is ever more important to use Scrum to tame this complexity.

In this chapter I will discuss what it means to run Scrum for multiple concurrent projects, as well as some specific techniques that make this possible.

What do you need to know to make it work? The first thing you need to know about running multiple projects is that you should never start with multiple projects at once. In fact, you should fear the complexity of such an environment and all of its evils. Imagine this:

changes to many application requirements,

business changes – changes in management, strategy, marketing, operations and business processes,

complex system setups to support a large number of concurrent applications:

clusters of servers working together,

complex dependency relationships among shared components,

ripple effects for changed component interfaces,

complex people issues:

project managers demanding attention to issues relevant to their project,

the need to migrate programmers across different teams,

lack of overall system knowledge,

turnover.

You get the idea? It can get to be very complex. However, this is precisely how companies live in an environment that promotes reusability among many projects.

7.1.1 The First Application

The first application is developed using the techniques discussed in the rest of the book. However, you may want to pay close attention to how you package the different components for the first project if you know there is a chance they will be reused by other projects. However, don't forget that your primary concern in the first application is to deploy it to production. You can always refactor and repackage components for a higher level of reuse later – after the release to production. So don't get too hung up in trying to make everything reusable from scratch – it just doesn't work very well to foresee everything. However, do use every opportunity you can to set things up so that reuse will be easier – this should always be a secondary concern in your first application.

Here are some ideas that can help you get ready for reusability:

Partition the architecture into layers. An example layered architecture for an online system will typically look like this:

Workflows – units of work linked together,

Units of work – components that include the front ends and the basic mechanics for requesting services and rendering onto presentations,

Business Service layer – reusable strategies,

Transactions – that compose a service,

Business Object layer – including all of its forms: value, business and data access objects,

Architectural Services: logging, security, persistence, distribution, concurrency.

Partition every layer into smaller packages that can be reused by other applications.

Keep close control on the external interfaces of these packages once their designs start "freezing" – stop changing.

At this point, the management of the application is still done through a single person, just as described in other parts of this book that talk about the management of single projects. But what happens when a second application group wants to build a second application using some of the resources that the first application produced? This requires some change, as we will see in the next section, because now - instead of having one Scrum team - we will have two and possibly three Scrum teams:

One team for each application and one team for the "shared resources".

7.1.2 Reusability

Very many developers and managers that work with new technologies touted as "reusable technologies" are accustomed to always working in the first release of an application. They tend to think that this is the most interesting part of development. The contrary is true – the interesting part of "reusability" starts to happen in the release of a second application and beyond.

The assumption here is that the first application has either gone into production or that it is very close to release to production. The key thing, and this is a strong prerequisite to start a second application, is that:

Whatever are chosen as "reusable assets" need to be **stable**.

If this is not true, there will be many problems. The application group that uses the shared components will complain that "things keep changing", and that the shared components lack the technical excellence they were told would be available for them. In some cases, and out of frustration, they will give up on using a shared component and develop their own. This might also create long-term problems based on lack of trust. On the other hand, the development group that develops the components will complain that they don't have the freedom to improve their components; they feel "pushed into a corner". They may possibly argue they are being forced to deliver something that wasn't intended for delivery.

My advice is simply: don't try to reuse anything that is not **stable** enough.

Another important assumption is that the first Scrum team will continue to develop and support future releases of the first application.

Based on these two assumptions a second Scrum team is formed with the idea to reuse some of the aforementioned assets developed by the first team.

7.1.3 Initial Setup and the Shared Resources Scrum Team

The Scrum Masters of both teams get together, including some of the upper management of both teams, and they agree to work sharing some components.

At this point, the **Shared Resources** Scrum team is created. Sometimes this can be avoided if the shared resources are small, or if the number of applications reusing the shared resources is one or two. However, if the shared components are medium to large, and the first Scrum team is small and/or has tight deadlines, a Shared Resources Scrum team dedicated to support the shared resources must be created. The initial resources of this team must include a mixture of some of the developers from the first application, and some new resources in order to prevent the complete depletion of talent from the first team. Sometimes this team is labeled as the "Architecture Team" but I strongly prefer "Shared Resources" team because it is more descriptive. But whatever name you decide, its responsibilities are very clear:

To support and enhance the shared components satisfying the requirements of multiple application teams.

The Shared Resources team might be just one person to begin with, and even a single person part-time. However, as the number of components and application groups supported increases, more resources will be needed to satisfy the development and support of the shared resources.

A key milestone of the initial process is to have the packages renamed and separated into a different package hierarchy. Depending on your development language and configuration management system, this means isolating separate packages into different projects so that they can be reused. This will cause the first application packages to change names, but typically these fixes are very easy to accomplish through a global search and replace utility.

From there on, the components isolated will be owned, supported and released by the Shared Resources team.

This initial setup can be done in conjunction with the development of the second application, but it is better to do it earlier rather than later. The danger is that if this setup is not done, the second application might just develop all of the components "all over again." Unfortunately this is often true, creating unnecessary expenses for companies.

The Shared Resources team also has the responsibility to coordinate and communicate changes to the shared resources. This might be difficult at times because the more applications that are dependent on shared resources, the more the "ripple" effect will be when changing the external interfaces of these components.

In general, start sharing components from the bottom layers of the architecture, such as the architectural services, and move through the layers until you reach the higher levels of reuse at the workflow level. In my experience, the different layers have different degrees of difficulty when shared:

The architectural services layer is easy to share – expect very little disagreement here.

The business object layer is difficult. There is typically some ambiguity and bias from applications to give special attention to abstractions that are more important for them. Resolve conflicts among the different application teams through hands-on meetings facilitated by an expert business object modeler.

The service layer is easy to reuse. It sits on top of the business object layers and typically uses the notion of "Strategies" [GOF]. The services are *always* taken from applications.

The "units of work" and workflow layers are easy. All units of work and workflows are *always* taken from applications.

Avoid the temptation of creating new business objects, services, "units of work", and workflows in the Shared Resource team. It is much better to abstract what is already built by another team and working. Similarly, create a new architectural service only when at least one application needs it. Don't ever create services that "in theory" will be used. This could be expensive and wasteful.

7.1.4   Developing the Second Application

Again, it is not required to do the initial setup described above before you start the development of a second application. However, it is strongly encouraged to be doing this at least simultaneously as the second application is started.

Developing the second application is essentially the same as developing the first application. The assumption that the second team with the internal shared components is the same as if they had bought these components off-the-shelf.

If the second application will also be contributing to the shared resources pool, use the same partitioning techniques that you used for the first application. When the intended shared components reach enough stability, then move them into a separate package and hand them off to the Shared Resource team. From then on, these components will be owned, supported and released by the Shared Resources team.

Just like in the first application, the second application's Scrum team has the primary responsibility of deploying their application. Their second priority is to think of reuse.

An important addition to the management practices is added at this point:

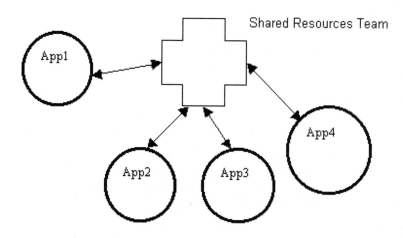

FIGURE 7.1: Multiple application environment.

It is a good idea to start meeting very often and regularly with the other Scrum Masters of the other applications and with the Scrum Masters of the support teams: Shared Resources, testing, and production support. These Scrum meetings are called "Scrum of Scrums", and I typically hold these meetings once or twice a week, and more often if needed.

One thing that is remarkable about Scrum is that it can in fact integrate very diverse teams like: 1) production support teams, 2) Scrum development teams, 3) XP development teams, 4) RUP development teams, 5) Mainframe development teams, 6) configuration management teams, and/or even 7) testing teams. In that regard, Scrum is unique in that it is able to provide a diverse number of teams an:

integrated and detailed management, estimating, planning and tracking process that can scale fairly well up to a whole business organization.

7.1.5   Developing More Applications

Essentially, repeat the steps described above in Section 7.1.2 "Developing the Second Application". Iteratively grow the architecture as you add more projects, each contributing with more and more shared components.

If you can run two teams sharing components, it is very likely that you can add more teams. But remember, if you plan to share components among very many different applications, you must setup a Shared Resources team.

7.1.6   Review of Specific Techniques

Let's review some of the techniques listed in this chapter:

Architecturally

Partition the architecture into layers

Partition every layer into components

Management techniques

Create a Shared Resources team

Hold frequent "Scrum of Scrums" meetings among the Scrum Masters

Reuse

Don't start sharing until components are stable

To begin reuse, package the components in a shared package and give the ownership to the Shared Resources team.

7.2   Applying Scrum to Larger Projects

Scrum works great for all project sizes but when applied to larger projects it requires some special considerations.

Large projects require careful thinking and planning when Scrum or any process is used. In this chapter I will provide some general guidance to tackle them. There is a strong similarity between managing a large project and managing multiple related projects. One consideration on why they are similar is reuse. In the case of multiple related applications, the reused components are the result of at least one application in production that now shares some of its resources with other applications. In the case of a large application, it is typical that multiple sub-teams work on the application simultaneously. Therefore, very similar rules apply.

7.2.1   The First Executable Prototype and First Branch of Development

First and foremost, don't try to get multiple units to do parallel development from day one. Parallel development, as said earlier, is difficult to accomplish, and while it apparently accelerates development, it can also bring many problems on its own.

Instead, first develop a minimal application that cuts through all the layers of the architecture using the techniques shown in this book, even if some of these layers are compromised. For example, you may not have a persistence service, or a transaction service, or a logging service ready; nevertheless, continue your development until at least one unit of work is ready. This minimal application may contain one or more entries from the product backlog and it is used to get the team warmed up. Even if this first release is not to be used in the real world, it is a good idea to jump all the necessary hoops as if the application will be released to production. This assumption helps resolve any issues with the development and release environments. Don't even try to do parallel development if the configuration management, testing, and release processes are not in place.

In small to medium applications it is easier to prioritize units of work according to their "business value" as said earlier. However, in large applications – especially if you want to do parallel development – the prioritization of the product backlog list has to also take into account the dependency among these units of work.

If at all possible choose a unit of work that has both high business value and uses a "root" domain object. By "root" domain object we mean a "fundamental anchor for your business and/or your application". In every business model there are a few objects or abstractions from which other objects or abstractions leaf. In a payroll system, for example, one cannot have employees without having persons first, and one cannot have payroll entries without employees. Person in this case is a root object because it leads to the definition of employees and employment that in turn lead to the definition of the branch. However, the person abstraction also leads to the definition of an indicative data branch that includes addresses, phones and email addresses; and the benefit plan branch, that in turn splits for different types of plans: 1) defined benefit (pensions), 2) defined contribution (401K), and 3) health and welfare (including medical, dental, and prescription benefits).

By partitioning a large application into several branches anchored into "root objects", large applications can be made identical to the "multiple related applications" practice described above.

7.2.2   Reusability

Eventually, as in the "multiple related projects" case, some abstractions will be candidates for reuse, and as I said earlier in the previous chapter:

Reusable assets need to be *stable*.

It is harder to predict reusability in general. It strongly depends on the application functionality and the domain model.

7.2.3   Initial Setup and the Shared Resources Scrum Team

It may take one or more branches in a large application to require a Shared Resources team. However, once a second branch is created the probability of reuse is very high if not for any other reason than for the reuse of architectural services: logging, persistence, security, printing, workflow.

Therefore, the creation of a minimal **Shared Resources** Scrum team is beneficial. As before the responsibilities of this team are:

To support and enhance the shared components satisfying the requirements of multiple sub-teams within a large application.

What happens when there are multiple applications and one or more are large applications? The rule then is to promote the release of shared components to the level that it makes more sense. If the components are only reused within a large application, then just promote them to the "large team shared resources team". However, if the components can be reused by more applications then promote the components to be released by the "Global Shared Resources Team."

7.2.4   Developing Through a Second Branch

The initial setup described above is a little bit more flexible in a large application; however, it is still strongly encouraged to let someone be the owner of the shared resources.

Because the branches have been decoupled, developing the second application is essentially the same as developing through the first branch. As the second branch is developed it may also contribute to the application's shared resources pool. Use the same partitioning techniques you used for the first branch. When the intended shared components reach enough stability, move them into a separate package and hand them off to the Shared Resources team. From then on, these components will be owned, supported and released by the Shared Resources team.

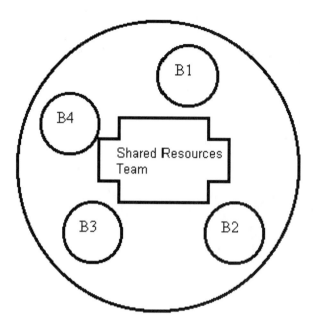

FIGURE 7.2: Large application with multiple branches B1, B2, etc.

Just like in the first branch, the Scrum team of the second branch's top priority is to deploy the application and their second priority is to think of reuse.

An important addition to the management practices is added at this point:

It is imperative to start meeting very often and regularly with the other Scrum Masters of the other branches as well as any support team Scrum Masters from the testing, integration, Shared Resources, and production support. These meetings are called "Scrum of Scrums", and they are held once or twice a week, and more often if needed.

7.2.5 Developing Through More Branches

Essentially, repeat the steps described above in Section 7.2.5 "Developing Through a Second Branch." Iteratively develop the application as you add more sub-projects. If you can run two sub-teams sharing components, it is very likely you can add more teams. But remember, if you plan to share components among many development branches within an application you must setup a Shared Resources team.

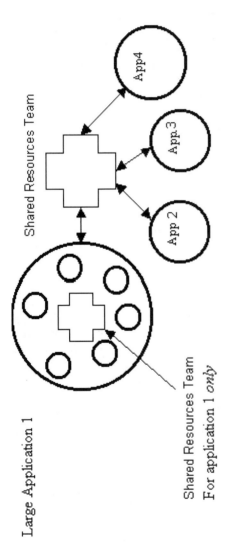

FIGURE 7.3: Large application in a multiple application environment

7.3   Case Study of Multiple-Related Projects: A Benefits Company

I'll now provide a case study of what took place at a benefits company over a period of nearly four years while the company launched its first e-commerce oriented web site and deployed a new family of web-based applications for its clients and internal users.

To summarize, in the end, the company developed 15 applications reusing many different components within the last year. However, it is not a story where everything went right from the beginning. Actually, almost quite the opposite happened. In retrospect, it is hard to imagine the outcome would be so bright after the first three years of web-development, because at that point the company had only one poorly developed web application in production. What happened in the last year that made the company successful?

The story started in late 1997, where the company's CIO directed the company towards e-commerce in order to offer prescription refills over the Internet. The first application deployment in late 1998 was successful but it was realized with a budget three times larger than planned and with a schedule twice as long as originally planned. Also, there were many technical concerns about the application.

However, the real problem was that five other business units were already lined up to develop web-based applications, with requirements to create up to 50 applications more within the next three years. But after the first web application, the IT department already had a bad reputation for taking a business unit's money and delivering late and over budget.

Frankly, the IT department at that point felt very scared. They had struggled to finish the first application, under the radar of all the top management in the company, and they weren't ready for more pressure. They did not feel they could develop that many applications in such a short time, especially since the budgets could not be enlarged. They felt pushed into a corner to deliver a *miracle*.

Parallel to the development of the first application, a so-called architecture group had been working on reusable architectural services components. It wasn't a coincidence that this group was created in early 1999, after the release of the first application. Its purpose was to create standard, reliable architectural services components so that other applications could be built over time – architectural services that in the first application released had a lot of problems. However, for political reasons, and in the name of "it is working, don't fix it", these services were not implemented in the first application until much later; actually, late 2000 as we will see later.

The application groups were told to wait to start development until the architecture team was done with the architectural services. But the architecture team was taking too long, so finally an application group agreed to co-develop the application while the architecture team finished all of the architectural services, which by then comprised a long and ambitious list.

The development of this second application started in mid 1999, but by late 1999, frustration started to show everywhere:

the application team members were complaining that the architectural services didn't work for them, and in some cases they either extended the services or just created their own.

the application team management was also getting frustrated and was blaming the architecture team management of being *careless and irresponsible*, because they allowed the interfaces of the architectural services to change often.

The architecture team, on the other hand, was frustrated to deliver what seemed *good architectural services*, but that the application team complained were either changing too fast, or simply not working correctly.

The highest point of frustration was reached probably in early 2000, when after failing many times to deliver on a scheduled date, the application team became both frustrated and fearful that the project would get canned and that the application team would be dismantled, or - in the worst case scenario - fired.

7.3.1   The Change in Direction

In May of 2000, however, my firm was contracted to help this situation. It was a desperate act of management to give it one last try. It was a "do or die" situation: either the effort would be successful within 3 months, or both the architecture team and the second application team would have to wait indefinitely. In the meantime, the company would stay with the legacy mainframe applications.

I recommended a short list of changes to be implemented:

Treat the architecture and the second application team as one team, and concentrate only on the delivery of that application.

Stop worrying about "reusable generic services" that may or may not be used, and concentrate only in what the second application needs.

Increase the feedback among all parties involved through the use of Scrum: application team members, architecture team members, production support team members and testing team members.

Stop worrying about documentation. Document the system after you go to production.

Find out a list of the minimal features that a production system will need and force both the application and the architecture team to work together on a daily basis to accomplish the work on that list.

The solution proposed was very radical and it caused many things to happen within the first month:

The official so-called "architect" of the system quit the project. Her primary reason was that she didn't have enough control over the architecture. However, with his departure, and without his explicit and draconian control, things started to move a lot faster.

The new "architect" allowed the architecture to be treated as if it were part of the application, meaning that everything in the architecture tasks was given priority in terms of the impact that it would have on the application schedule.

All documents other than the code, the user's guide, and the production support documents were stopped.

A list of essential features was created through a Product Backlog, and a Sprint Backlog was created for a Sprint.

The new architect and his new team were immediately assigned to work in pairs with the developers of the application.

Scrum meetings were held every morning at 9 am; this caused:

Team members to show up on time.

Team members to acknowledge their true status.

Team members to get familiar with what others were doing and the problems they were having. This caused the whole team to get an overall *sense of urgency.*

Management to resolve issues. During the first weeks it was noticeable that management wasn't involved in the project as much because they kept reporting – more than anyone else, the same status. By the end of the second week the most embarrassed team members were the production support manager and the testing manager who had not been able to establish the production and testing environments.

After only 1 month, a very imperfect release emerged. Everyone was excited. By working together the tension between the application team and the architecture team had decreased – they were in it together after all. Even some people dedicated to update the Rose diagrams in the architecture team had stopped documenting, and participated in the bug fixes. Actually, the Rose diagrams went untouched from there on, because everyone was much more excited about actually releasing code to production.

However, the system was still not in production. After a quick demo to management, a new planning meeting took place to choose the next wave of Product Backlog and the remaining bug fixes in the previous Sprint Backlog. The second release (after only three weeks) in early August provided an implementation of most functionality. And the final Sprint – the one that delivered the system to production in early September, mostly solved bugs.

We had actually missed the "end of August" deadline imposed by management to cut-off the project by seven days but by now top management saw results and they were pleased.

7.3.2   The Second Application

Meanwhile, I organized the second team and a newly created third team to follow in the first team's footsteps:

Choose a minimal list of features and create Sprint Backlogs;

Work with the architecture team by "pairing" resources to resolve issues and develop features; and,

Take the attitude of "servicing" the application teams within the architecture team.

The second application was released in later October. And the third application was released in January of 2001.

7.3.3   More Applications

As of the summer of 2001, there are ten applications in production using the same technology, five more under development to be released before the end of the year, and from fifteen to twenty five more scheduled to be delivered over the next two years. The third application team got a company wide award for its performance. They developed a fairly large application, involving dozens of screens and CICS transactions in only five months, with at least three-quarters of their team being retrained mainframe developers. What a contrast from the first few years of development!

7.4   Case Study of Large Project: An Outsourcing Company

In the spring of 1994, I got involved in a large software development project to outsource benefit management operations. Its goal was to implement software for 1) defined benefit (DB) plans like pensions, 2) defined contribution (DC) plans like 401Ks, and 3) health and welfare (HW) plans. Its primary goal was to replace an IBM mainframe-based system implemented with on-line CICS, assembler, COBOL, VSAM and IMS.

Customer service representatives and clients would continue to be the primary users of the software. The new 3-tier system was to be developed using Power Builder and VRUs (voice response units) on the presentation tiers, C++ on the middle tier, and Sybase and the legacy data stores on the backend.

Apart from the old technologies used - which were seen as a dead-end for the company's technology strategy - the old system was perceived as being very expensive, because the implementation of every client required new code. The methodology for the implementation of a new client was basically: 1) copy the code of the client that best fits the description of the new client, and 2) tweak as needed for the customer ad infinitum. Instead, the new system proposed to only implement the *differences* found from the base system and whatever a new client needed. In theory it would save a great deal of money to the company. An existing client that was willing to be the guinea pig drove the first implementation of the system. The risk to this client was minimal since their benefits program was outsourced anyhow, and there was a backup plan to continue its outsourcing with the mainframe system should anything not work as expected.

It was a good business plan. However, something went wrong with the software implementation. The first release was planned for January 1st, 1995, but that didn't happen. These are some of the characteristics of the project:

It took a very long time to gather all of the requirements up-front.

It took a very long time for the architecture to be *defined* in paper by the so-called architects of the system. In the meantime there were 30 coders waiting for their designs.

It took a very long time to develop the ability to do configuration management, testing and release management.

There was little or no communication with the customer.

There were excessive layers of management.

Most everyone was demoralized, overworked and frustrated and no one really believed in the project plan anymore. In fact, it used to be the center of jokes and sarcastic comments.

The organization kept changing organizational structure: from sub-system driven, to phase driven, to tier driven, to client driven, going around in circles.

By the summer of 1995, almost 2 years after the project had been started there wasn't even a single piece of functionality that ran end-to-end for the first customer. Then a second customer was signed-up. You could see *fear* in the eyes of people, who asked themselves "If we can't finish with one customer, how do they (marketing) dare to sell another one?"

By now, the project had consumed 30 million dollars and at its peak had 80 staffers and 80 consultants working full-time. The company was facing the possibility of lawsuits and had already paid high fines for not delivering the system to the first client in the first year, and was facing more fines for the first client and the second client, if the system was not delivered by January 1st, 1996.

By August of 1995, there was an incredible amount of staff turnover. Almost everyone that had worked on the first client was bailing out of the sinking ship, and new resources were interviewed and hired almost daily. The only problem was that there was an estimated three-month learning curve for the system; basically, the new resources would be actually useless for the 1/1/1996 release.

Despite this situation, and desperate to save the company's division from going bankrupt, I and a few other managers and technical resources proposed in late August to write the application for the second client using a different strategy. We would select ten of the best people in the organization, hire ten new ones and create a "small team" environment. We were tired of failing using the "rules" of the organization but we still believed in ourselves. It was very evident that neither the stiff processes, nor expensive tools, nor the beautiful Gantt charts we had used so far would help us.

I gathered some of the existing techniques to manage small to medium size teams and we chose org patterns and the Scrum techniques to manage our project. Org patterns had been recently published in the proceedings of the first two pattern conferences and Jeff Sutherland had recently announced Scrum in the OTUG (object technology user's group) mailing list.

So in early September, equipped with our newly found friends, we had our first "Sprint Planning meeting." We chose to implement the "indicative data" section of the application that included beneficiaries, their addresses, phones and basic plan information. This functionality was what was promised to the client by January 1st, 1996. We created a backlog that broke this functionality in assignable chunks. However, one of the key differences of Scrum was that it allowed Backlog items other than functional requirements. This made a tremendous difference because we could see for once the "hidden tasks" that we had left out by blindly making our plans "use case driven." We chose to have only two Sprints of about two months each. We chose to implement only indicative data in the first Sprint, and to implement plan information in the second Sprint.

Even before we had our first Sprint planning session, we started meeting every morning at 10 am for 15 minutes to hold the Daily Scrum meetings. These meetings kept us focused on what we were doing and they kept constant score on what was being done. They also allowed us to manage and expand the Backlog according to our needs. Our Backlog was kept as an Excel spreadsheet that included:

what was required to be done,

what was the priority of the work,

who was responsible if the item had been assigned,

a rough estimate of how long would it take to complete,

an entry for who had created the Backlog entry.

At the Daily Scrums items were either removed from the Backlog, changed status, or were added. We soon found out it requires quite a bit of discipline to run the Scrum meetings and to keep track of the issues. I acted as Scrum Master and struggled to keep the list in synch.

Our first iteration was a booming success. For the first time in two years we had produced something that actually executed and everyone was very excited. Our second iteration delivered our application on time for release to production, but we struggled a lot for this delivery. However, this struggle showed us what Scrum was really capable of. Scrum integrated all of the management tasks into managing the Backlog, and that included backlog items for everyone in the team including testing, production support, release management, configuration management, and of course software development. This feature of Scrum was perhaps the most beneficial.

Nobody could believe it. We had done with about twenty people what couldn't be done with 200 in the previous two years. And remember that half of the twenty were new hires.

The following year, we put four more releases in production, and we had expanded the number of concurrent Scrum teams to three. One Scrum took care of the conversion, another one was still dedicated to indicative data, and a third one was dedicated to pension calculations.

Before the first release to production, this division of the company was considering losses. A year later, it was a profitable operation.

CHAPTER   8

Scrum And The Organization

Most organizations aren't optimized for productivity. Scrum helps
them to optimize, freeing employees to do their best and removing
impediments to productivity.   —

8.1   Organizational Impact

Scrum can be used to re-engineer an organization so that it is more productive. Organizations are rarely optimized for productivity. As they grow
and mature, inefficiencies accumulate. Just as fat slowly accumulates and
clogs human arteries, slowing the flow of blood through the heart, inefficiencies accumulate and clog the organization's arteries, slowing everything
down. An informal organization arises within the formal organization. The
people who are said to "know how to get things done" are the people who
know how this informal organization works. These people know how to
function effectively within both organizations, and for this reason, most
successful managers have a few people like this on their staff. However,
this is an inefficient way to boost productivity. It makes more sense to
solve the underlying problems.

Many people come to work and are faced with obstacles they have to
surmount before they can start working. As they work, they spend much of
their time removing additional obstacles. They try to get out of meetings,
they try to get purchasing to hurry up and get some needed software, they
have to meet with personnel to go over a new review policy, and they are
called into a status meeting. Not only do all of these obstacles take time,
they interrupt the ability of a team and its members to focus on work.
People need to get their minds around a problem, discuss it, and come up
with the best way to solve it. The opportunity to do so at work is pretty
rare.

Scrum makes obstacle removal an objective. The Scrum Master is
responsible for listening to obstacles and removing them. Scrum tries very
hard to free people to be productive, to do their very best, by providing
uninterrupted time when they can work.

Scrum offers organizations the opportunity to identify obstacles to
productivity. At every Daily Scrum, impediments to work are identified
and plans are made to remove them. These impediments rarely represent

isolated incidences of inefficiency within the organization. Rather, they are usually part of a larger problem. Scrum is constructed so these impediments are highlighted, day after day, until they are resolved. This is called "bottom-up process re-engineering," because the impediments are actual problems hindering important development projects. This type of process re-engineering is based on actual need.

At the Daily Scrum, the team is asked if there are any impediments to performing its work. This question is not regularly asked in most development projects, and these projects accumulate impediments like a ship accumulates barnacles, until there are eventually so many impediments on the project that it is hard for the project to make any headway. The most formal impediment identification mechanism I'd heard of before Scrum was called the "project post mortem." At the post mortem, after the damage is already done, management met with the team to identify what could have been done differently. Too little, too late.

Once a team identifies an impediment, it expects the impediment to be removed. A team assumes that if someone is asking if there are impediments, he or she is going to do something about the impediments. If management doesn't remove the impediments quickly, Daily Scrums grow progressively more demoralizing. They eventually become embarrassing. If management does not remove impediments, it becomes clear that it cares so little about the project that it would rather accept productivity loss than help the team. If management cannot or will not remove the impediments that are reported, then it sometimes makes sense to recommended that the Sprint be cancelled.

One of the most important responsibilities of managers is making sure that productivity remains as high as possible. Scrum provides management with a daily glimpse at productivity levels and the factors that are affecting them. It gives them a sort of managerial cheat sheet: a list of ways in which management can increase productivity. What an opportunity! Here is a chance for management to both remove the impedances forever and to help the project succeed. Every time managers hear the word "impediments," they should think "opportunity."

8.2   Impediment Example 1

The organization had a number of projects underway that would together build the next release of an Internet news service. A senior engineer writing C++ needed a library from RogueWave Software and requisitioned it from purchasing. During the Daily Scrum, the Scrum Master noticed that she kept bringing this up as an impediment. The Scrum Master knew that if she called RogueWave, the library could be delivered the next day. For some reason, she had already waited four days, and during this time, a key piece of software wasn't being developed.

The Scrum Master did two things. First, the Scrum Master immediately removed the impediment by calling RogueWave and buying the software. The engineer was productive the next day. Then the Scrum Master went to purchasing to find out what the hold up had been. There was one person doing purchasing work, and this person was wrapped up with the quarterly financials. Purchasing was backed up, and the Scrum Master recommended that additional help be hired during this busy time period.

8.3   The Scrum Master as a Change Agent

Who is responsible for removing impediments? The answer is the entire organization. The Scrum Master takes charge of the impediments, assuming responsibility for working with everyone in the organization to remove them. But the whole organization has to be committed.

The Scrum Master runs the Daily Scrums, is in touch with all aspects of the project, and is responsible for ensuring that impediments are removed. The Scrum Master needs to have management's full support and engagement. Most importantly, the Scrum Master needs to have the authority to cause impediments to be removed. If management disagrees with actions that the Scrum Master takes, it should offer suggestions, provide guidance, and give coaching. But no matter what, management must support the Scrum Master. In the previous example, management supported the Scrum Master's decision to acquire the RogueWave software library and promptly reimbursed the Scrum Master for the out-of-pocket expenses.

Empowering the Scrum Master to remove impediments is a touchy subject. An impediment is something that is putting a damper on productivity. If an organization welcomes these opportunities and appreciates the efforts of the Scrum Master, Scrum is operating as it should and productivity increases. However, attempts to remove impediments do not always go over well. Sometimes organizations have accommodated impediments for so long that they are unwilling to remove them. For instance, the head of purchasing might react negatively when the Scrum Master tries to have a problem in purchasing fixed. In some companies, the Scrum Master in the above example would have been criticized for not going through purchasing and for not following standard procedures.

A friend of mine asked, "How would this work in a large centralized purchasing department where change was nonexistent due to implementation of SAP, for instance?" The Scrum Master could still expense the software to immediately resolve the impediment. Then the organization would have an example to test the effectiveness of the SAP implementation in purchasing. Was the new purchasing process reducing productivity? If so, how could it be improved?

Scrum causes change. Organizations that implement Scrum should expect to enjoy greater productivity and the ability to produce regular, competitive releases. However, they should also expect to incrementally reengineer themselves. Scrum offers a great opportunity for increasing an organization's productivity. However, the Scrum Master needs to know what authority he has to rapidly resolve impediments. If the answer is "not much," then maybe the organization in question isn't ready to implement Scrum. This may provide an opportunity to reflect on the organization's priorities and on the balance between organizational stability, flexibility, productivity, and competitiveness.

8.4   Impediment Example 2

Complex, n-tier software was being built for delivery of products across the Internet at a company. As new engineers were added to the team, personnel would notify purchasing, which would acquire equipment and software according to standards set by a vendor. However, the standards were over a year old, and developers were trying to develop using multiple windows on 15-inch monitors. The engineers accepted them because they thought 15-inch monitors were what management had selected. Management's attention was focused elsewhere, and no one in management was aware that there was a problem.

During the Daily Scrums, the Scrum Master often heard about engineers using two workstations at once: one for development, and another obsolete workstation for email and office applications. The engineers had "requisitioned" second workstations from departing employees. This was very inventive of them; they were using available resources to solve their problem. However, the use of multiple workstations inevitably led to overcrowding. When the Scrum Master investigated the situation and found its root cause, the Scrum Master immediately contacted the vendor so that the team would only receive large monitors. The Scrum Master then worked with management to bring the workstation standard up-to-date and to make it easier for engineers to modify the workstation standard when necessary.

8.5   Impediment Example 3

A team was readying a tunable laser subsystem for an important electronics show. Two senior engineers were in charge of engineering the subsystem. Other members with less optical physics experience were handling the programming, parts assembly, and board preparation. During the Daily Scrum, the senior engineers kept talking about how much difficulty they were having obtaining parts. The subsystem was absolutely cutting-edge technology, so they had to procure very advanced components from other manufacturers. Telephone tag was consuming most of their time, breaking their concentration, and delaying the arrival of critical components.

The Scrum Master equipped the senior engineers with cell phones and reassigned a junior engineer to take the lead in understanding and procuring components. The Scrum Master had to use an engineer because of the complexity of the procurement and the amount of engineering discussion that had to take place for procurement to be handled correctly. Whenever a question arose that he couldn't answer, the junior engineer would call the senior engineers on their cell phones, resolve the question, and continue the procurement process.

8.6   Keep Your Eyes Open

Daily Scrums make team dynamics more visible, and the team learns to use them to discuss gripes, or impediments. Management must listen not only to the explicitly stated impediments, but also to the general conversation prior to and after the Scrum. Impediments that the team has come to think of as "our company's way of doing business" are often discussed then. Listen closely and think about what you're hearing at these Daily Scrums. Patterns emerge from conversations, jokes, and ribbings that lead the astute observer to find hidden impediments that everyone takes for granted. Remove them and make the team more productive.

8.7   Impediment Example 4

During one project the Scrum Master noticed that the engineers kept getting up and going to other cubicles to discuss what they were doing. The organization had everyone except senior managers in cubicles and wasn't amenable to an open workspace environment. Since the team was formed dynamically, the cubicles weren't adjacent, and the engineers had to break their concentration to get up and walk over to someone else's cube, who very well might not be there. With the participation of systems administration (cabling and phone extension changes), the Scrum Master moved the team so everyone was adjacent to each other. Then the Scrum Master put chairs by the cubicle walls, so team members could see over the cubes to ask questions and discuss design issues. Suddenly, the team's work area looked like a prairie dog town, heads popping up as team members worked more effectively with each other.

The productivity from rearranging the cube assignments resulted from astute observation by the Scrum Master. Rather than accepting everything as a given, the Scrum Master was driven to do anything to make the team's life easier, to make them able to be more productive.

8.8 Impediment Example 5

Each team member reported at the Daily Scrum that they had no impediments. However, for the last day they had been working on peer reviews, and they would be continuing to work on them for the next two days. The organization had a semi-annual review process when everyone who has worked with an individual is required to complete a "Peer Review" form. These were fodder for the individual's manager in completing the review. Since everyone worked with most everyone else, each individual had to complete at least five, and sometimes more than ten, peer review forms.

Everyone on the team saw this as a normal part of working at that company. The Scrum Master saw it as an impediment. This hadn't been planned into the Sprint Backlog and it had nothing to do with completing the project. The Peer Review process was an organizational responsibility, rather than project imperative. And the team members were used to organizational responsibilities taking priority over their project responsibilities. The Scrum Master got the team back on their project work and requested that management defer the Peer Review process until after the Sprint.

8.9 Organizational Encroachment

I worked at Wang Laboratories during its golden years (1980-1984) and during the start of its calcification (1985). Wang was growing rapidly during this time, and people were being hired left and right. As Wang grew, a lot of support functions were delegated to newly created support organizations. Soon senior vice presidents, who had vice presidents, directors, and managers reporting to them, headed these support organizations, like personnel and purchasing. They spent their time researching and developing policies, procedures, forms, and protocols that were imposed on the rest of the organization. Everyone had to follow these, since otherwise they'd be bucking the Senior VP. It became easier to do the organizationally imposed work than to see what was reasonable. Work gave way to bureaucracy. Initiative gave way to stagnation. This, of course, isn't the full story of Wang's demise by any stretch of the imagination. But it certainly did cause a lot of productivity loss to my projects.

Scrum, through the impediment identification, provides a way for management to become vividly aware of this organizational encroachment on productivity. Everyone griped about Peer Review, but accepted it and kept going. However, as a result of it being highlighted during the Daily Scrum, management was primed to see the consequences and take action. The whole review process was rewritten by line management *with the support of personnel*, into something much more streamlined and appropriate.

8.10   Impediment Example 6

During the Daily Scrum, the Scrum Master noticed the team members were counting their change. When questioned, they disclosed that they were determining if they had enough change to buy coffee. They had chosen to work late to deepen some functionality, and they wanted coffee to keep sharp. However, there was only one coffee machine on the floor and it required $.85 in exact change. In desperation, the team members sometimes had to hunt down the janitors and borrow change from them!

The Scrum Master had never worked anywhere that didn't provide either inexpensive or free coffee to its developers, so the Scrum Master was baffled by this oversight. The Scrum Master figured he would remedy this immediately, because it was a no-brainer, a slam-dunk, something with impact and little effort. The Scrum Master called the facilities manager and told her that the team needed coffee, and what would she recommend? She indicated that the company had coffee previously, but everyone griped about it. She had gotten tired of their complaints, and now there was no free coffee. The Scrum Master was aghast, and protested that if the team wanted to take caffeine to stay awake and write alert code, the least the company could do was provide the caffeine for free. The facilities manager retorted that this was a family company and it didn't want to encourage indulgence in drugs that kept the engineers away from their families. Then she went ballistic and informed senior management that Scrum was undercutting company values!

Whew, that was a workout just to get coffee. Eventually, coffee worked its way back into the organization, but each time with reference to when the Scrum Master got his head handed to him over a cup of coffee.

8.11   Scrum and Mission Statements

Organizations have mission statements. For example, a provider of healthcare information systems has the following mission statement:

"XXSYS uses information technology to maximize value in the delivery of healthcare — by improving the quality of patient service, enhancing medical outcomes, and reducing the cost of care."

Everything an organization does probably should be in support of this mission, or be explained, or the mission revised to accommodate exceptions. Anything that an organization values that impedes that mission should probably be stated. For instance, in the infamous case of the free coffee, that organization's mission statement would have to be modified as such:

"XXSYS uses information technology to maximize value in the delivery of healthcare — by improving the quality of patient service, enhancing medical outcomes, and reducing the cost of care, unless the employees need coffee."

C H A P T E R   9

Scrum Values

Scrum is based on a set of fundamental values. These values are
the bedrock on which Scrum's practices rest.   —

As I've described Scrum, I've also described some of the values, or
qualities, that the people using Scrum display – commitment, focus, openness, respect, and courage. These values all emerge as people participate in
Scrum. Scrum teams are asked to take initiative, to wrestle with complex
requirements and technology. To do this, the team must learn to rely on
itself. During a Sprint, no one external to the team tells the team what to
do. The team has to figure it out on its own. It may have to go up blind
alleys, to make compromises, or even fail. But the team and its members
have to be forthright and resolute as they attempt to do their work and
meet their commitments. This section demonstrates how Scrum values
emerged at a startup medical products company, MedImp (an alias for a
real company).

Medimp produces an innovative product that allows healthcare professionals to capture healthcare charges and view laboratory results on a
handheld computer. Several healthcare institutions were successfully using its products. Servers that synchronized the information to the handheld computers with healthcare institution's legacy systems were supplied
and managed by MedImp. Consequently, when the healthcare institution
signed up for MedImp's products, MedImp would bring servers into the
institution, interface them, and then monitor and control them from Med-
Imp. MedImp was an application service provider (ASP) to the healthcare
institution.

I was brought in during mid-2000 as MedImp's sales and implementations started to ramp up. MedImp needed to deliver servers to new accounts
while improving the total product reliability, availability, and sustainability
(RAS). MedImp had recently formed a Systems Engineering team to take
on this work. Their job was to build an ASP system that could deliver adequate RAS to the customer. My job was to show them how to use Scrum
to continue delivering systems to customers while they improved RAS.

9.1 Commitment

> Be willing to commit to a goal. Scrum provides people all the
> authority they need to meet their commitments.   —

Most of us have trouble standing up and saying that we'll commit to something. We've learned from experience that it's often best not to. Scrum has practices that support and encourage commitment. For instance, the team has the authority to decide how to do the work it's selected. The notion that a team of people will have absolute autonomy and full authority to do its best is novel in most organizations. Most employees are used to being told what to do and how to do it. At first, people are distrustful and do not believe that management will let Scrum operate this way. But once people start experiencing empowerment, they begin to have faith in their leaders and even in themselves.

When I arrived at MedImp, the systems engineering team was trying to improve the product's reliability, availability and sustainability (RAS). Every time a system at a customer site crashed, the team struggled to get it back up again. Since the systems were at remote locations, the team wanted to be proactive. Its goal was to notice that a system was going down before the customer called.

The team was firefighting existing problems while trying to improve RAS within the existing ASP model and determine the proper long-term solution. The team's first step had been to upgrade to dual-CPU Compaq servers. Its second step was to review offerings from vendors of monitoring, control, and backup/recovery solutions. When I arrived, it was in the middle of assessing solutions from many vendors.

I instituted Daily Scrums and became the Scrum Master. I immediately saw a major obstacle to committing to adequate RAS. "Adequate" hadn't been defined! The service contracts didn't specify the performance or the availability of the MedImp offerings. Because there was no stated goal, the customers and management expected adequate to be perfection, the absence of any problems. The systems engineers didn't know if adequacy entailed 99% reliability 24x7, or 90% only during the hours when the customers were using the system. Since the team didn't know the RAS target, it didn't know which vendor offerings were appropriate. I quickly escalated this issue to management and determined that the team had to support 99.9% availability per month only during the shifts when the customers were using the product.

The second issue in determining the right ASP solution was price. Some of the vendors offered solutions that were quite expensive, and would raise the price per ASP system by over $30,000. No one knew if this was acceptable or not, since no one had a pricing model to use for various size institutions. Was a $100,000 solution acceptable to a 50-user healthcare institution, or would a $20,000 solution be more appropriate? The prior model had simply been "as inexpensive as possible." Management revised the pricing model, establishing a "high water mark" to support 50 users that was $50,000 in capital costs. The team also had to take scalability into account. The RAS model had to scale with the pricing model. Users expected fees to decline with volume, so RAS costs had to similarly scale downwards.

The team now had the requirements and could commit. It needed to build an ASP solution that was 99% available during shifts when the system was being used and which had an installed cost of less than $50,000. Its job was to design, test, and start implementing a solution that met these criteria. The team was able to quickly focus the vendors on these requirements. Many of the solutions were too expensive, some of the solutions provided inadequate RAS, and some vendors just didn't have Linux products.

9.2   Focus

> Do your job. Focus all of your efforts and skills on doing the work
> that you've committed to doing. Don't worry about anything else.
> —

Producing a valuable product increment out of somewhat vague requirements and unstable technology is hard work. It requires attention and focus. The problem needs to dominate our thoughts, to fill our mind; all of our time at work should be consumed by our attempts to solve the problem. Once we are focused, all of our time is spent looking for and trying solutions to bring order to the problem. People who are attracted to building systems and products like to fix problems. Scrum lets a team set up problems and provides them an environment in which it can focus. But old habits are hard to break, and most of us are used to accommodating distractions. There are so many things to do at work. We are fodder that other people use to fill their days, and we use other people as fodder to fill up our own days.

The systems engineering team at MedImp was under the gun. It had committed to meeting RAS and pricing targets with an ASP solution that it designed. In every engineering problem, there are four constraints: cost, time, quality, and functionality. RAS represented the quality constraint. Implementation schedules driven by sales represented the time constraint. Functionality was variable so long as RAS was met. The cost of engineering the solution was also somewhat flexible, although I learned that it was difficult to increase our engineering costs since engineers were impossible to find and the fees were astronomical during this time period, the latter half of the year 2000. Most available systems engineers were skilled in Sun/Solaris using Oracle, but MedImp's existing ASP model used Compaq/Linux and Oracle. MedImp tried to find engineers who had experience with Intel and Linux architectures, but they couldn't be found, experienced or not, full time or contracted. The team wasted a great deal of time interviewing people who professed to have, but actually didn't have, the needed skills.

The team wasn't focused on the problem. It was spending all of its time maintaining existing ASP implementations and interviewing people. During the Daily Scrums, I noticed increasing frustration. How was the team going to meet its commitments if it didn't have the people? While discussing this problem, several of the systems engineers bemoaned the fact that they weren't using Sun/Solaris solutions. Their backgrounds were in Sun/Solaris. More talent was available on the street with Sun/Solaris skills. Why couldn't the team use Sun/Solaris? Then it hit them! The team had the authority to figure out how to meet its commitments. If it could design an acceptable ASP model using Sun/Solaris, that was fine! The result was that the team shifted to a Sun/Solaris solution. By doing so, not only did it draw on existing strengths and skills, but also it was able to utilize engineering talent available from Sun resellers and distributors. MedImp was also able to find Sun/Solaris engineers that could be contracted. The team was able to increase engineering costs to meet quality and time requirements, even in a desperately tight job market.

There are so many other distractions at work. Email is a big one, particularly with the "cc" feature and with mailing lists. Employees arrive in the morning to find a full mailbox that needs to be tended. During the day, all sorts of interesting email arrives. Commercial conversation groups provide even further distraction; they provide sounding boards for ongoing arguments and discussions about everything from raising kids, to skateboarding, to building computer systems. The team found that it was best to start "filtering" its email, most importantly all "cc" emails. The founders of the company, who came from an academic setting, loved the intellectual dialogues that these emails promoted, and the team had felt that - to live up to company expectations - it had to participate. I gave them "permission" to skip the participation, and the amount of email dropped to an acceptable level.

One of the finest Scrum Masters I've ever worked with had a saying: "What's that got to do with code?" She applied this rule unfailingly at Daily Scrums, thereby helping teams learn to focus on the task at hand. With time, this type of focus becomes ingrained and team members naturally deflected distractions.

9.3   Openness

Scrum keeps everything about a project visible to everyone.   —

Scrum keeps everything open and visible. Openness is required for Scrum to work, and Scrum mechanisms help foster this openness. Product Backlog, for example, is visible to everyone. Daily Scrums keep visible what a team is working on. The results of a Sprint are visible during the Sprint Review meeting. And work trends and velocity are made visible by tracking remaining work across time. Scrum removes the ability to dissemble. Responsibilities are clear, authority is allocated, and everything is visible.

While the Scrum team was Sprinting, management requested some team members to investigate and pursue an IBM solution. I immediately detected this distraction in the Daily Scrum when someone complained, "We can't meet with EMC to look at its Sun compatible storage solution because there's an IBM meeting!" I told them to skip the IBM meeting. The team learned that it has the right and the authority to meet its Sprint commitments. How it meets these commitments is up to them.

One Scrum practice that counters interference is the rule that no one is allowed to add work to a Sprint once it is underway. Once the MedImp team was underway, and the ASP model problem was being solved within defined constraints, no one was allowed to add work to the team's backlog by changing the nature of the ASP model problem. I've found this type of distraction to be particularly true in start up organizations because so many options are being explored at once. If the team can't stay with its commitments, the product just won't get out the door. People and teams spend their time chasing one option after another, and not much of anything gets produced.

It is better to produce something than it is to pursue many alternatives, please everyone, and produce nothing. The IBM partnering alternative was very attractive (and eventually selected), but the team was Sprinting to mold a Sun/Solaris solution. As Scrum Master, I asked management to decide whether to cancel the Sprint or not, because the IBM work was outside of the Sprint's backlog. If management had selected to cancel the Sprint, we could have redefined another Sprint to include the IBM work, but then the team probably couldn't have committed to delivering much of an improvement to RAS. Management agreed to ask IBM to proceed on its own, and instructed the team to continue the Sprint.

9.4 Respect

> Individuals are shaped by their background and their experiences.
> It is important to respect the different people who comprise a
> team.   —

First, management staffs a team. These are usually the best people
who are available. Scrum then establishes an environment in which these
people can work together as a team. Every individual has his or her own
strengths and weaknesses, comes from a unique background, and is trained
and gains skills through a unique history of education and employment.
Mix these individuals into a team and it gains the strengths of team dynamics. You also can anticipate prejudice, resentments, petty squabbles,
and all of the other negative attributes of human relationships. Stir into
this mix the difficult technology and emerging requirements of today's software industry and problems will undoubtedly occur.

Dave was hired to be the Oracle systems administrator in the systems
engineering team at MedImp. The team had committed to a Sprint goal.
Dave had assumed that the Sun/Solaris implementation of Oracle would be
similar to the IBM implementations that he had administered at previous
jobs. Unfortunately, Dave found that the tricks he had learned for IBM
didn't work on Sun/Solaris. Dave had also never implemented a solution
on a fault-tolerant EMC I/O subsystem using RAID 5. Dave struggled to
keep up with the database administration work he had committed to, but
he fell further and further behind.

The other systems engineers started to feel that Dave was slowing
them down. They had to help him with his work so they could progress
with their work. As their work suffered, they began to resent him. Dave
felt this and started to come in to work later and later in the day, not
wanting to face what he perceived to be his inadequacies. But Dave was
quite adequate. Dave was faced with a mix of requirements and technology
that was beyond his skills to solve in the allotted time. His fellow team
members weren't happy about the possibility that the team might fail to
achieve its goals, and they had found in Dave a convenient, if undeserving,
scapegoat. We all have seen this kind of situation. It sometimes gets out
of hand, and inevitably ends when the team loses Dave.

People are not used to working in self-organizing teams. By "self-
organizing," I'm referring to the team's adjusting and adapting to meet its
commitments for a Sprint. Although management has selected the team
members, Scrum leaves the actual determination of who does what up to
the team. The team self-organizes not only at the beginning of a Sprint,
but continually as work progresses throughout the Sprint. Since it is the
team as a whole that commits to the Sprint goal, the team is going to

sink or swim together. There are no individual heroics, just team heroics. When a team member is weak, other team members have to pick up the slack. Nothing helps people do their best, despite their shortcomings, as much as group pressure and a team environment.

Since the team had settled on a Sun/Solaris solution, Dave was doing his best. But he was frustrated to find that his skills weren't readily portable to the Sun/Solaris platform. The team needed good database administration. Because Dave was unable to provide what the team needed, the team felt that Dave was letting it down.

Scrum is empirical. The team can always reduce functionality or increase costs (if the budget allows) to meet its goals. Dave's job wasn't getting done. What could we do? Dave hadn't experienced Scrum before and didn't know that he was empowered to figure out how to meet his commitments. I posed this question to Dave – what was he going to do to meet his commitments? After brainstorming with the whole team about his options, Dave exercised his authority and brought in an Oracle database administration consultant to help and train him. Luckily, he was able to quickly acquire the services of one such consultant from a Sun reseller. The point the team learned from this was not to focus on what couldn't be done, but instead to brainstorm about how it could meet its commitments. These individuals had committed as a team, and so they needed to work together as a team. There could be no individual failures, only team failures.

It is important to do your best, to remember everyone else is doing his or her best as well, and to help your teammates whenever you can. After several Sprints, teams learn each other's strengths and weaknesses, accept them, and learn how to accommodate them and compensate for them.

9.5   Courage

> Have the courage to commit, to act, to be open, and to expect
> respect.   —

Few people come from a work environment with Scrum values. Although empowerment is a trendy word, most organizations are still hierarchical and authoritarian. For a team to act differently requires courage. I am speaking of two kinds of courage: the courage to find out that the environment will support these values, and the courage to be willing to find out that relying on one's own judgment is acceptable – even laudable.

Courage in Scrum isn't a visible, tangible thing. It is not some kind of romantic heroism. Instead, it is having the guts, the determination, to do the best you can. It's the stubbornness not to give up, but to figure out how to meet commitments. This type of courage is gritty, not glorious. Dave's courage was the willingness to openly admit that he needed help and to ask the rest of the team to help him figure out what to do. The courage went a step further when he assumed the authority to do something about his needs. I saw Dave vacillate for several weeks. Sometimes I'd see Dave fuming and blaming himself for not being "good enough." I helped Dave stand back and understand that he had authority to figure out how to fulfill that responsibility. Dave figured out how to rely on his initiative and wits to devise solutions to his problems. Dave learned that the only person who could decide how to do his work was Dave himself.

Scrum isn't for everyone. But it is for those who need to wrestle working systems from the complexity of emerging requirements and unstable technology.

Bibliography

[Agile]   Fowler, M. and J. Highsmith, *The Agile Manifesto*, Software Development, **9**(8): 28-32, 2001.

[Crosby]   Crosby P., *Quality is Free: The Art of Making Quality Certain*, Mentor Books, 1992.

[DeGrace]   DeGrace P. and Stahl L. H., *Wicked Problems, Righteous Solutions: A Catalogue of Modern Software Engineering Paradigms*, Englewood Cliffs, N.J., Yourdon Press, 1990.

[Dennett]   Dennett, D. C., *Darwin's Dangerous Idea: Evolution and the Meanings of Life*, New York, Simon & Schuster, 1995.

[Fowler]   Fowler, M.,*Is Design Dead?*, Software Development **9**(4), 2001.

[Goldratt]   Goldratt E., *The Goal: A Process of Ongoing Improvement*, North River Press Inc., Great Barrington, MA, 1992.

[Harris97]   Harris M., *Culture, People and Nature*, Addison Wesley Longman, New York, 1997.

[Holland95]   Holland J., *Hidden Order: How Adaptation Builds Complexity*, Addison and Wesley, Reading, MA, 1995.

[Holland98]   Holland J., *Emergence: From Chaos To Order*, Addison and Wesley, Reading, MA, 1998.

[Kauffman93]   Kauffman S., *The Origins of Order: Self-Organization and Selection in Evolution*, Oxford University Press, Oxford, 1993.

[Kuhn]   Kuhn T., *The Structure of Scientific Revolutions*, The University of Chicago Press, Chicago 1970.

[Levy]   Levy, S., *Artificial life: The Quest For A New Creation*, New York, Pantheon Books, 1992.

[McConnell]   McConnell S., *Rapid Development*, Microsoft Press, 1996.

[Miller]   Miller G., *The Magical Number Seven, Plus or Minus Two*, Psychology Review, 1956.

[Peitgen]   Peitgen, Jurgens, and Saupe, *Chaos and Fractals, New Frontiers of Science*, Springer Verlag, 1992.

[ScrumPattern]   Beedle M., Devos M., Sharon Y., Schwaber K., Sutherland J., *Scrum: A Pattern Language for Hyperproductive Software Development*, Pattern Languages of Program Design, Harrison N., Foote B., Rohnert H. (editors), Addison-Wesley, 4: 637-651, 1999.

[Senge]   Senge P. M., *The Fifth Discipline: The Art and Practice Of The Learning Organization*, New York, Doubleday/Currency, 1990.

[Takeuchi and Nonaka] Takeuchi H. and Nonaka I., *The New New Product Development Game*, Harvard Business Review (January 1986), pp. 137-146, 1986.

[Takeuchi and Nonaka] Nonaka I., Takeuchi H., *The Knowledge Creating Company: How Japanese Companies Create the Dynamics of Innovation*, Oxford University Press, Oxford 1995.

[Tunde]   Ogunnaike Babatunde A. and Harmon Ray W., *Process Dynamics, Modeling and Control*, Oxford University Press, 1994.

[Wegner]   Wegner, P., *Why Interaction Is More Powerful Than Algorithms*, Communications of the ACM **40**(5): 80-91, 1997.

[Weinberg]   Weinberg, G., *Quality Software Management (all volumes 1-4)*, Dorset House, 1992-1997.

Index